BestMasters

Springer awards „BestMasters“ to the best master's theses which have been completed at renowned Universities in Germany, Austria, and Switzerland.
The studies received highest marks and were recommended for publication by supervisors. They address current issues from various fields of research in natural sciences, psychology, technology, and economics.
The series addresses practitioners as well as scientists and, in particular, offers guidance for early stage researchers.

Kim Leonie Kellermann

The Impact of Minimum Wage Regulations on Educational Incentives for the Youth

An Empirical Analysis for Germany

Foreword by Prof. Dr. Thomas Apolte

Springer Gabler

Kim Leonie Kellermann
Münster, Germany

BestMasters
ISBN 978-3-658-16488-1 ISBN 978-3-658-16489-8 (eBook)
DOI 10.1007/978-3-658-16489-8

Library of Congress Control Number: 2016958519

Springer Gabler

Printed on acid-free paper

This Springer Gabler imprint is published by Springer Nature
The registered company is Springer Fachmedien Wiesbaden GmbH
The registered company address is: Abraham-Lincoln-Str. 46, 65189 Wiesbaden, Germany

Foreword

The introduction of a generally applicable minimum wage in Germany was accompanied by a vigorous academic and public debate. While the majority of the general public welcomed the reform, considerable concerns were brought forward by the academic community. The concerns focused primarily on direct effects on the realm of employment. The discussion of indirect effects only amounted for a small part of the overall debate, even though these effects can be substantial.

The present master thesis was submitted by Kim Leonie Kellermann at the Chair of Political Economy at the University of Münster in December of 2015. The aim of the thesis was to analyze the incentives regarding educational decisions of the young population resulting from a generally applicable minimum wage. While the theoretical approach of the thesis is plausible, it is not unequivocal. Provided that a minimum wage is legally binding, it improves the income of low-skilled workers. This in turn reduces the wage gap in comparison with high-skilled workers. Conversely, however, if a binding minimum wage results in unemployment of the low-skilled workforce, it might as well increase educational incentives.

The net effect of these two partial effects can only be assessed empirically, and this constitutes the central task of Kim Leonie Kellermann's thesis. She achieves this task on a level that can stand comparison with research papers published in high-ranking outlets. The methodological approach and the econometric estimations are convincing without exception and reflect the state of the art of empirical analysis in this particular field of research. The results and conclusions that Kim Leonie Kellermann draws from her analysis are just as persuasive.

It would have been a waste if such an outstanding and at the same time highly relevant work had vanished in the archive of the university's examination office. That is why it is all the more gratifying that Springer Gabler included this thesis in its series BestMasters. I would like to express my sincere gratitude to the publishing house. I offer the thesis and the insights developed therein my best wishes for broad dissemination.

Prof. Dr. Thomas Apolte

Acknowledgements

I was lucky to receive fundamental academic support in writing this master thesis. First of all, I would like to thank my supervisor Prof. Dr. Thomas Apolte for enriching the project by proposing new ideas and drawing my attention to alternative ways of analyzing the problem. I am also truly grateful to my co-supervisor Lena Gerling of whose expertise in empirical research methods I benefited very much. Furthermore, special thanks go to Helena Helfer and Dr. Thomas Ostertag for frequent scientific and methodological discussion about various research projects at that time.

Beyond that, I am obliged to all my friends and family who supported me both regarding the thesis and personally. I give many thanks to Sebastian for successfully solving all software problems and helping to put this thesis on paper. Finally, I owe sincere thanks to my parents who motivated me and cheered me up during this challenging time.

Kim Leonie Kellermann

Contents

List of Tables

List of Figures

List of Abbreviations

CAA	Collective Agreement Act
CBA	collective bargaining agreement
CL	conditional logit
DIW	Deutsches Institut für Wirtschaftsforschung, German Institute for Economic Research
GLS	generalized least squares
EU	European Union
FSO	Federal Statistical Office
GSOEP	German Socio-economic Panel
IIA	independence of irrelevant alternatıves
ISCED	International Standard Classification of Education
MIL	mixcd logit
MLSA	Federal Ministry of Labor and Social Affairs
MWL	Minimum Wage Law
NACE	Nomenclature statistique des activités économiques dans la Communauté européenne
NSE	not in school but employed
NSNE	neither in school nor employed
OECD	Organization for Economic Cooperation and Development
OL	ordered logit

OLS ordinary least squares

PWA Posted Workers Act

SE in school and employed

SNE in school but not employed

1 Introduction

Ten years after the last widespread institutional reform (cf. Eichhorst/Marx, 2011), the German labor market has experienced another fundamental public intervention in 2015: since January 1, the first nation-wide statutory minimum wage has been in use (cf. Minimum Wage Law (MWL)). The great majority of workers is now eligible for a gross hourly wage of at least 8.50 €. Further increases will be realized in 2017 at the earliest (cf. §§ 1, 9 MWL).

Hardly any political measure has been attended by a comparably controversial and polarizing debate in politics and media. On the one hand, left-wing and social-democratic parties as well as employees' representants greatly welcome the regulation (cf. German Green Party, 2013, pp. 88-101; German Social Democratic Party, 2015; German Trade Union Confederation, 2015; Palier/Thelen, 2010). During the past decades, studies have illustrated the constantly widening wage gap in Germany (cf. Dustmann et al., 2009; Müller/Steiner, 2009). The number of low-income workers who have to rely on additional public support has risen. Especially after the *Hartz Reforms*, public critism has been arousing about a marginalization of the *working poor* whose wages are too low to support themselves (cf. Eichhorst/Marx, 2011; Palier/Thelen, 2010).

In order to ensure that working incentives persist and to prevent the creation of a secondary low-wage labor market, a state intervention has been considered necessary (cf. German Trade Union Confederation, 2015; Müller/Steiner, 2009). A major argument of minimum wage proponents is social fairness: every active worker who makes a contribution to social welfare should be shown profund appreciation in terms of an appropriate wage level. Furthermore, a legal wage floor reduces the mentioned income gap which results in higher social equality (cf. German Social Democratic Party, 2015; German Trade Union Confederation, 2015; German Green Party, 2013, p. 89). Wage minima allow for a worthy lifestyle without depending on state transfers, thereby lowering respective public expenses (cf. German Social Democratic Party, 2015; Palier/Thelen, 2010).

However, the opponents of the statutory minimum wage who are composed of conservative politicians and employers' associations consider it to be a severe danger to Germany's position in the global economy. As a high wage country, a further rise of labor costs bears the risk of a shrinking international competitiveness (cf. Confederation of German Employers' Associations, 2014). Prior to the passage of the legislation, the pressure of massive lay-offs caused the greatest concerns. Workers whose productivity does not match the imposed wage floor are unattractive employees for profit-oriented firms and the inevitable consequence of dismissals was annouced. The affected low-skilled individuals would then pose another burden on the social insurance system. Thus, a marginalization is not avoided but rather promoted by a minimum wage (cf. Bauer et al., 2009; Confederation of German Employers' Associations, 2014; Knaab/Schöb, 2008). Moreover, employers feel overwhelmed by the documentary obligation laid down by the MWL. In their opinion, too much costly additional work is demanded as they have to deliver information on working hours and payments to the Ministry of Labor and Social Affairs (MLSA) in order to control the minimum application (cf. § 17 MWL; German Trade Newspaper, 2015).

A notable point is that this debate mainly focusses on wages and employment. Special emphasis is placed on immediate reactions which become visible after a short period of minimum use. However, considering the respective scientific literature, other impacts have been studied. One issue that is even addressed by the German legislation is the educational effect of minimum wages. Increasing wage prospects set higher incentives for youths to leave the educational system or abandon a low-paid professional training program in order to earn the higher minimum with a full-time employment (cf. Neumark/Wascher, 2010, p. 192; Amlinger et al., 2014; Möller, 2014). Since the public aim is to support the acquisition of further skills, the MWL declares the potentially concerned groups ineligible for the wage minimum. Thus, under-aged workers who have not completed a vocational training so far are exempted as well as youths doing an apprenticeship (cf. § 22 MWL; Federal Ministry of Labor and Social Affairs, 2015a).

Again, this exception has been criticized: workers' representants declare the inapplicability of youths devaluating for the MWL pursues the goal of a general provision of fair wages (cf. § 1 MWL; Amlinger et al., 2014). Furthermore, abstracting from social argumentation, the exception design does not fit the German labor market structure: most youth workers and apprentices are full-aged and thereby applicable for the minimum which sets incentives to switch to full-time employment before having obtained a professional degree (cf. Möller, 2014; Schulten/Horn, 2014). While several simulation studies have been conducted to reveal potential employment effects of the statutory minimum wage, no analysis of educational effects has been performed yet (cf. Möller, 2014).

Therefore, this master thesis is concerned with the question of educational impacts of minimum wages in Germany. The main goal is to enrich the discussion about the necessity and adequacy of the current exceptions by empirical evidence that is lacking so far. The investigations provide information on a potentially disincentivizing effect which could be prevented by an exemption. To do so, an empirical analysis is conducted in order to determine the effect of longer-existing sectoral wage floors on the decision of 17- to 24-year-olds to undergo professional training. With the help of micro level data from the *German Socio-economic Panel* (GSOEP) and added data on minimum wages and the labor market situation, a mixed logit model covering the years 1994 to 2013 is estimated. The observed effects are used to evaluate the youth exemptions from the statutory minimum wage regarding the mentioned points of criticism.

Section 2 introduces the subject of minimum wage effects on education by a review of the existing literature. First, the theoretical considerations exposed by the Human Capital Theory are presented. The main purpose is to understand the conceivable educational reactions of labor market agents facing a wage floor. The reflections have been scrutinized in various empirical studies of which an overview is given afterwards. The observations are summed up and crucial deductions with respect to the empirical framework in this thesis are drawn. Section 3 then sheds light on the different forms of minimum wages in Germany that this thesis refers to. Special emphasis is placed on sectoral minimum wages, their fixing procedure and application. In a second step, the new minimum regulation is presented in more detail. The youth exceptions are further explained and the launched discussion about their constructional adequacy is outlined. Thereby, the main questions to answer during the empirical analysis are clarified.

Following this, in section 4, the analysis is designed. The methodological approach is illustrated considering the included dependent and independent variables. The set of appropriate regression techniques for discrete choices is reasoned whereas a mixed logit model serves as the baseline approach. Moreover, the dataset in use is introduced. By looking at descriptive statistics and stylized facts, an impression of data features and potentially interesting findings are given. After this preparatory work, the regression results are provided in section 5. In addition to the baseline specification, several robustness checks examine the stability of the observations.

Section 6 is then concerned with the interpretation of the obtained evidence. Underlying reasons and differences to the previous literature are discussed. In a last step, the evidence is linked to the minimum wage exemptions of youths in order to enhance the respective debate by empirical findings. Furthermore, the limiting aspects of the analysis are taken into account, inspecting the reliability of the estimation results. Based on this, room for further investigations is motivated. Section 7 finally concludes.

2 State of Research

As to evaluate minimum wage impacts on education, the relation between income and skill acquisition is clarified first. The theoretical background is illustrated by the *Human Capital Theory*. Building on this, possible educational reactions of labor supply and demand to a wage floor are discussed. Later, a presentation of various empirical studies follows which serve as a point of reference for the empirical analysis carried out in this thesis.

2.1 Theoretical Foundations

Since the 1960s, the heterogeneity of work and its causes have taken on greater importance in economic theory. Workers have been recognized as imperfectly substitutable since they exhibit different levels of skills and productivity. Thus, at least in the long run, firms do not only choose the optimal quantity but also the optimal quality of work (cf. Cahuc/Zylberberg, 2004, pp. 173-176). To illustrate how differences in skills emerge, the role of education and the economic motivation for its acquisition have been investigated (cf. Becker, 1964, p. 1; Schultz, 1981, p. 46). The crucial step was made by Schultz and Becker who developped the Human Capital Theory. Of the one part, different wage levels can be explained as a result of non-equal productivities in a free market (cf. Cahuc/Zylberberg, 2004, p. 251). The Human Capital Theory reverses the causality: expected future wages given a certain productivity set incentives to obtain the respective level of education prior to labor market activities (cf. Becker, 1964, pp. 1-2; Schultz, 1981, pp. 11-12; Cahuc/Zylberberg, 2004, p. 69).

In the following, education is understood as a form of practical and/or theoretical training serving to expand individual skills, especially those usable for occupation. Professional education in Germany is institutionalized by the *apprenticeship* system that offers a combination of compensated practical training and supportive schooling leading to a vocational degree (cf. Büchel, 2002; Franz/Soskice, 1995). While apprenticeships have originally been used in trade industries only, they have been established for the majority of occupations up to the present (cf. Franz/Soskice, 1995). The respective training is publicly regulated with regard to learning objectives, examinations and worker protection (cf. §§ 4, 17, 34 Vocational Training Act (VTA)). For a detailed description of the apprenticeship system, see Franz/Soskice (1995).[1]

Becker names the individual amount of abilities and knowledge *human capital* (cf. Becker, 1964, p. 1). To understand its economic value, one can parallelize its accumulation to that of physical capital and treat educational choices as investments: a higher level of education increases productivity and thereby future wages. Thus, a low-skilled individual seeking to maximize income and utility[2] has an incentive to enlarge her human capital stock by participating in an educational activity (cf. Checchi, 2006, p. 19). Let U be a representative individual's working lifetime utility function depending only on lifetime earned income Y:[3]

$$U = U(Y). \tag{1}$$

For simplicity, $q = l, h$ represents the only possible skill levels. At the beginning of her working life, the individual is on the lower skill level l. She can either remain there and earn the corresponding market wage W_t^l or become a high-skilled worker by undergoing an educational activity in period $t = 0$. Afterwards, her wage is W_t^h with $W_t^h > W_t^l$.

1 Although this article has been published twenty years ago, it is still frequently cited as a source of general information on the German apprenticeship system.

2 For simplicity, it is assumed that income is entirely spent on consumption which is the only source of utility. There is no disutility from work and there are no public instruments, e. g. taxes or transfers. Furthermore, human capital is not depreciated.

3 The analytical illustration of the optimization is based on Becker (1964), pp. 9-13, 30; Checchi (2006), pp. 18-23 and Cahuc/Zylberberg (2004), pp. 173-175.

Similar to a physical investment, the individual has to bear the coss of education first whereas the benefit in terms of a higher wage W_t^h will only be realized in future periods $t = 1, 2, ..., T$. These cost are twofold: by assumption, the optimal amount of work time H_0 has to be spent on training completely. Thus, the individual foregoes the gainable low-skilled wage W_0^l. In addition to these opportunity cost, each unit of education involves direct cost C, e. g. material cost or tuition fees (cf. Becker, 1964, pp. 30, 37-38; Checchi, 2006, pp. 21-22). The individual weighs the total cost of education and the present value of future benefits. If the latter is greater, the educational investment is made (cf. Schultz, 1981, p. 12). Y, given an investment in education in period $t = 0$, a market interest rate r and a discount factor β is stated as

$$Y(H_t) = \sum_{t=1}^{T} \beta^t \frac{W_t^h}{(1+r)^t} H_t - (C + W_0^l)H_0. \tag{2}$$

Following eqs. (1) and (2), the individual maximizes lifetime earned income with respect to work time H_0, H_t it

$$\sum_{t=1}^{T} \beta^t \frac{W_t^h}{(1+r)^t} = C + W_0^l, \tag{3}$$

that is if the marginal utility from education equals its marginal cost (cf. Becker, 1964, pp. 38-39; Checchi, 2006, p. 18). What has to be kept in mind is that – despite the analogies – an investment in human capital differs from an investment in physical capital in one pivotal point. Human capital is an inseparable part of the individual and cannot be sold. For that reason, individuals encounter barriers when seeking to finance investments in education. Due to the unsaleability of human capital and the missing security for lenders, individuals might fail to receive a loan. They are prevented from education although it would be worthwhile undergoing from a point of view of utility maximization (cf. Becker, 1964, pp. 56-57; Checchi, 2006, pp. 19, 49, 117). For that reason, the acquisition of skills is positively correlated with family wealth: being able to rely on parental income, youths from richer families do not have to forego education in case of lacking loans (cf. Checchi, 2006, pp. 29-30). Eq. (3) furthermore illustrates why (professional) skills are usually acquired at a young age. The further away is the end of working life in period T, the longer time remains for an educational investment to pay off (cf. Becker, 1964, pp. 50-51; Mincer, 1974, pp. 8-9).

Queuing Hypothesis Against the backdrop of minimum wages, special emphasis is placed on the outlined trade-off between future wages and cost of education. The introduction of a minimum wage $MW_t > W_t^l$ marks an external intervention on the labor market (cf. Cahuc/Zylberberg, 2004, p. 714). Normally, minimum wages are binding for a certain fraction of the labor force, i. e. there exist a number of low-skilled workers that earned less than the minimum wage before (cf. Neumark/Wascher, 2010, p. 50).[4] The higher income opportunities change the optimization displayed in eqs. (1) to (3). By lifting the legal wage floor above the market wage for the low-skilled, the opportunity costs of education increase.[5] With cost exceeding future benefits, the optimality condition in eq. (3) is not balanced anymore. The individual refuses to take part in further education but prefers to work for the minimum wage (cf. Ehrenberg/Marcus, 1982; Checchi, 2006, p. 23; Neumark/Wascher, 2010, pp. 50-51):

$$\sum_{t=1}^{T} \beta^t \frac{W_t^h}{(1+r)^t} < C + MW_t. \tag{4}$$

Labor supply in the low-skilled domain rises and an excess supply causes unemployment to increase. The negative minimum wage effect on human capital is even enlargened then. Not only that the stock of human capital is not extended because of foregone educational

4 A minimum wage that is not binding for any worker is assumed to have no consequences for the labor market situation.

5 The direct cost of education C are assumed to be unchanged as well as the market wage for high-skilled workers $W_t^h > MW_t$ which is a simplification.

activities, it is diminished as being out of practice reduces the value of skills used for production (cf. Becker, 1964, pp. 8-9; Schultz, 1981, p. 35).

This potential outcome of individuals looking for employment instead of undergoing education is termed *Queuing Hypothesis* (cf. Neumark/Wascher, 2010, p. 51). It appeals to young individuals in particular: having just left school, youths have not participated in occupational education yet. Moreover, their professional experience is lower than of older workers. Consequently, young labor market entrants are mostly low-skilled (cf. Acemoglu/Pischke, 1998) and likely to be affected by a minimum wage. Thus, they prefer a direct entry into full-time employment facing high opportunity costs of education (cf. Neumark/Wascher, 2010, p. 208; Campolieti et al., 2005).

Substitution Hypothesis The described processes reason the government's aim to counteract the negative minimum wage effects on education. Nevertheless, another outcome is conceivable. The Queuing Hypothesis only reflects the labor supplier's educational decision. Basically, a wage floor also affects the behavior of labor demanders which in turn has an impact on workers again. As mentioned above, employees are paid according to productivity. Leaving out capital as an input factor[6], the representative firm with a profit function

$$\Pi_t = P_t F(L_t^l, L_t^h) - \sum_{q=l,h} W_t^q L_t^q \tag{5}$$

realizes a profit maximum if

$$P_t[F'(L_t^l) + F'(L_t^h)] = W_t^l + W_t^h \tag{6}$$

where L_t^l, L_t^h are the respective quantities of low-skilled and high-skilled labor hired and P_t is the given market price for output $F(L_t^l, L_t^h)$. If the minimum wage is exogenously

6 This is again to simplify the analytical considerations.

fixed above the market wage for low-skilled workers, $MW_t > W_t^l$, the costs of employing them rise. Unsurprisingly, profit-maximizing employers only keep those workers whose marginal productivity is at least equal to the legal wage floor. Instead of deploying low-skilled workers at the minimum wage, employers substitute them with high-skilled labor. They reduce L_t^l and raise L_t^h until eq. (6) is in balance again (cf. Cahuc/Zylberberg, 2004, p. 173; Campolieti et al., 2005; Ehrenberg/Marcus, 1982). Because of this shift in labor demand, the probability of being employed ρ_q declines for the low-skilled. Transferring this aspect to the educational decision, eq. (3) is modified for workers affected by the minimum to get:

$$\rho_h \sum_{t=1}^{T} \beta^t \frac{W_t^h}{(1+r)^t} > \rho_l(C + MW_t) \tag{7}$$

The actual probability to find a job is taken account of: due to the reduced labor demand, low-skilled workers cannot fully be sure to be employed, therefore $\rho_l < 1$. Thus compared to eq. (3), the opportunity costs of education fall because of $\rho_l < 1$ given the same minimum wage raise.[7] With a strong drop in demand for low-skilled labor, the low probability of being employed outweighs the higher wage. The marginal utility of education now exceeds its marginal cost. Low-skilled individuals are encouraged to undergo additional training in order to improve their employment prospects (cf. Neumark/Wascher, 2010, p. 207; Agell/Lommerud, 1997). Following the fact that this outcome is induced by employers substituting low-skilled with high-skilled workers, it is referred to as the *Substitution Hypothesis* (cf. Neumark/Wascher, 2010, p. 51; Ehrenberg/Marcus, 1982). With respect to education, it produces a positive effect contrary to what results from the Queuing Hypothesis.

Based on these explanations, two major findings can be stated. First, it is not possible to clearly predict the educational effect of minimum wages (cf. Neumark/Wascher, 2010, p. 209). According to the two theoretical outcomes, the case of a declining level of edu-

7 Moreover, it is $1 \geq \rho_h > \rho_l$ as the probability of being employed is larger for high-skilled workers.

cation is plausible as well as the case of an increasing level. This ambivalence suggests to empirically analyze which effect is observed in reality. Second, the bidirectional causality between wages and education is partly settled with a minimum wage. With an endogenously determined market wage, causality runs in both directions. The skill level of labor suppliers determines the market wage which in turn sets educational incentives for labor market entrants and thereby shapes the future average skill level (cf. Cahuc/Zylberberg, 2004, p. 69). However, a minimum wage that is fixed outside the market can be assumed to influence the educational decision while the reverse causality is less likely to emerge: as the introductory controversies have illustrated, wage floors are purposely fixed above the current low-skilled market wage to raise income. The at least partial absence of endogeneity enables to formulate a clear relation between the variables. The following section presents major empirical studies in this field and their results. Furthermore, a closer inspection of methodological approaches provides information on considerable aspects to include in the upcoming empirical analysis.

2.2 Evidence of Minimum Wage Effects on Education

2.2.1 Negative Impacts of Minimum Wages

The great majority of studies concerned with the relation of minimum wages[8] and education comes from the U.S. Minimum wages date back to the beginning of the 20th century there and American researchers were the first to reflect about their educational impact (cf. Neumark/Wascher, 2010, pp. 9-10, 12-15). Mincer/Leighton (1980) link the Human Capital Theory to wage floors and outline the resulting decline of employers' willingness to finance on-the-job-training.[9] At the beginning of a new employment, a worker is open

8 In the following, the term *wages* refers to gross hourly wages unless otherwise stated.

9 The Human Capital Theory intensively discusses the provision of on-the-job-training by employers (cf. Becker, 1964, pp. 7-28). In this thesis, the main subject is formal professional education. However, since the German apprenticeship system involves employer-financed on-the-job-training, the respective considerations are relevant to some extent.

to participate in job-specific training. Since this is costly for the employer, the worker will not receive the full wage according to his productivity but a reduced amount (cf. Mincer/Leighton, 1980). However, this reduction is impossible when being forced to pay a legal minimum wage. Therefore, initially low-skilled workers for which the wage floor is binding are not offered any training because employers cannot apportion the cost. On the contrary, initially high-skilled workers are not affected by the legislation. They take part in firm-specific training and even enhance their productivity. The decline of job training opportunities particularly applies to school-leavers with only compulsory education due to their still low skill level. Thus they will expand their human capital stock at their own charge in the formal educational system if they can afford to stay there. Later when they enter the labor market as higher-skilled individuals, they are paid a wage above the minimum and have good prospects to receive further job training (cf. ibid.).

To support their argumentation, the authors perform a linear panel regression analysis[10], concerning the question of whether the probability of receiving job training falls with a minimum wage. They use various household survey data covering the periods from 1967 to 1971 and from 1973 to 1975 and estimate separate effects for ethnic and skill groups. The results confirm the theoretical conclusions: minimum wages have a negative effect on the probability of participating in job training for initially low-skilled workers, reducing it by about 2.2 percentage points. In contrast, there is a small increase of 0.1 percentage points for initially high-skilled workers whose education goes beyond high school level (cf. ibid.).

Subsequent studies rather focus on formal educational choices, i. e. schooling of youths face to minimum wages. Ehrenberg/Marcus (1982) establish a study design which is frequently reused in later studies: limiting their data to a sample of U.S. teenagers aged 14 to 19 in 1966/1968, they estimate a *multinomial logit*[11] model in order to determine the

10 Their approach is not further specified.

11 Greene (2012) briefly addresses the problem of the ambigous use of this term for both variants of a logit model with and without individual-specific regressors (cf. Greene, 2012, pp. 801-802; Wooldridge, 2010, pp. 497-499; Borooah, 2002, pp. 2, 72). Following his classification, the logit

probability of choosing a certain occupational activity from a discrete set of alternatives. The dependent variable is the individual's enrollment-employment status with four mutually exclusive manifestations: an individual can either be in school and employed (SE), in school and not employed (SNE), not in school and employed (NSE) or neither in school nor employed (NSNE).[12] The minimum wage variable is constructed in two stages. First, the hourly state minimum, relative to the hourly state average, is adjusted for the minimum coverage rate. In a second step, family backgrounds are considered: if family income, adjusted for family size, is equal or greater than 8000 $ per year, a teenager's family is classified a high-income family. If family income is equal or below 4000 $, a family is classified a low-income family. The minimum wage variable interacts with the respective dummies indicating the income classes. Teenagers from middle-income families are omitted. Furthermore, several control variables are included, such as gender or previous education, none of which is examined in detail (cf. Ehrenberg/Marcus, 1982).

The cross-section estimation is conducted separately for sexes and ethnicities. The results meet the authors' expectations: with a 10 percentage point raise of relative minimum wages, the probability of SE increases significantly by 6.1 percentage points for white boys from high-income families and decreases by 2.1 percentage points for non-white boys from the same background. If non-white from low-income families, boys face an even higher reduction in probability of SE of 4.8 percentage points. In line with that, the probability of NSE increases by 5.4 (5.2) percentage points for white (non-white) boys from low-income families (cf. ibid.). The overall probability of schooling increases for boys from wealthier, white families and decreases for those from non-white, low-income families. The opposite is the case regarding the probability of employment. For girls, most estimates are insignificant. The authors' interpretation is as follows: in case education is affordable for a teenager's family, a minimum wage induces further schooling. If a

model for discrete choices including both alternative- and individual-specific regressors is referred to as the *conditional logit* model while the term *multinomial logit* describes a model with individual-specific influences only.

12 Being SE means that schooling is the major activity and a teenager works part-time beside school (cf. Ehrenberg/Marcus, 1982).

family is less wealthy, minimum wages set higher incentives to enter the labor market (cf. Ehrenberg/Marcus, 1982). This finding matches the theoretical suppositions made by the Human Capital Theory (cf. section 2.1) and by Mincer/Leighton (1980). Furthermore, educational choices obviously vary with gender, ethnicity and family background, suggesting an influence of heterogeneous tastes or social inequality.

The estimation method is adapted by Neumark and Wascher (1995a). In their first empirical work with respect to education and minimum wages, a panel analysis is carried out based on state level micro-data from the U.S. Current Population Survey for the years 1977 to 1980. They take over the four-category dependent variable specifying a *conditional logit* (CL) model with state and year effects. The minimum wage variable is the coverage-adjusted ratio of the hourly state minimum to the respective state average. Both the current and the one-period lagged values enter the estimation. A vector of controls consists of several demographic variables (cf. Neumark/Wascher, 1995a). The authors find that a 10% increase in relative minimum wages results in a reduction in size of the group enrolled in school by 3.4%. Concurrently, the proportion of NSNE teenagers increases by 6.7%. The net effect on teenage employment is slightly negative but insignificant. Consequently, the observations are interpreted in favor of a substitution behavior of employers: since the net employment effect is nearly zero, few jobs for youths are cut by the mininum wage. Obviously, teenagers who have been in school until the minimum wage raise are now in demand on the labor market. They replace the lower-skilled with less formal education who are then categorized NSNE (cf. ibid.). The authors succeed in further supporting their results by a second study in 1995. Here, they also compute the transition probabilities from one employment-enrollment category to another. Again, they find a negative enrollment effect. Furthermore, the impact on the probability to go from no schooling to schooling is negative as well, reflecting the fact that teenagers who lose their jobs do not return to the educational system. Additionally, youths having received a wage below the minimum are likelier to be dismissed in the course of a rising wage floor than those whose wages have been above (cf. Neumark/Wascher, 1995b).

In 2003, Neumark/Wascher replicate the results for the periods from 1978 to 1989 and from 1980 to 1998. The minimum wage effect on schooling probabilities remains negative while the effect on the probability of NSE is positive (cf. Neumark/Wascher, 2003). The substitution of workers is moreover confirmed by studies analyzing the individual employment effect of a minimum wage in particular. Currie/Fallick (1996) estimate the probability of holding one's job in the next year for workers facing a binding minimum wage. The estimated effects using a linear probability model are significantly negative. In addition, the authors briefly report their attempt to estimate the reverse probability of unemployed persons returning to the labor market which is also negative (cf. Currie/Fallick, 1996). As it is more difficult for workers bound by the minimum wage to find an employment, this is a sign of a smaller demand for low-skilled work and a possible determinant of educational decisions.

The same direction of effects is also observable using aggregate measures of education. Chaplin et al. (2003) construct a schooling continuation ratio: for a predefined area, the current number of students in a specific grade is divided by the number of students in the previous grade one year before. This method provides information on the share of students who continue schooling in the following year. The authors work with data on grades 9 to 12 and on high school graduates. Here, the absolute values of state minimum wages are used, nonetheless, the authors control for inflation and the average manufacturing wage on state level. As the legal compulsory schooling age varies among U.S. states, dummies are interacted with minimum wages to control for permission to leave school under the age of 17, at the age of 17 or at the age of 18 (cf. Chaplin et al., 2003). Running a panel OLS regression with state and year effects, a significantly negative effect is observed for students who can drop out of school at the age of 16 already: the continuation ratio declines by roughly one percentage point if the minimum wage increases by 1.00 $. To test for sensitivity, the model is estimated separately for all grade-to-grade transitions. Again, the minimum wage effect is significantly negative regarding the transition from grade 9 to 10 with a legal school leaving age of 16 or 17. No significant effects are observed in states with a higher compulsory schooling age and for higher grades respectively (cf. Chaplin et al., 2003). First, this is evidence of the fact that students are willing to work at a higher minimum wage but are held back by law. Second, students who are close to finishing high school are intent to graduate and are therefore not discouraged by minimum wages. One can deduce, as a thoughtful policy implication, that negative effects on formal education can partly be counteracted by a high compulsory schooling age.

As mentioned earlier, empirical evidence from other countries is not as large as from the U.S. In a study of Canadian youths, Landon (1997) finds negative educational effects of minimum wages as well. Based on Canadian provincial data covering the period from 1975 to 1989, he estimates the enrollment rate, i.e. the proportion of 16- and 17-year-olds enrolled in school relative to the total of the respective age group. In line with previous studies, a relative minimum wage on province level is included as exogenous regressor. In addition, there are control variables reflecting schools' and labor market characteristics, e.g. student-teacher ratios, provincial expenses per student and provincial unemployment rates. The panel OLS estimation is conducted for each sex and age group. In all specifications, a significantly negative effect of a relative minimum increase can be observed except for the group of 16-year-old girls. Using the estimated coefficients, a decline of the enrollment rate by about 1% is predicted for all age groups if the province minimum wage is raised by 0.50 $ (cf. Landon, 1997).

Two more recent studies have revisited the topic by looking at minimum wage effects in New Zealand. Pacheco/Cruickshank (2007) also measure the level of education by school enrollment rates between 1986 and 2004. They rely on a broader cohort consisting of individuals aged 16 to 24. As the minimum wage in New Zealand is of general type, differing only between under-agers and adults, absolute values are used. The results of a panel least squares analysis indicate an insignificantly negative effect of minimum wage raises (cf. Pacheco/Cruickshank, 2007). Splitting the sample into teenagers (16-19 years) and young adults (20-24 years) yields a negative effect on enrollment for the younger group and an insignificantly positive effect for the older group. As an explanation, the authors state that young adults who already finished school or even a professional training are less likely to be affected by a minimum wage compared to lower-skilled teenagers. Thus, the latter face a higher incentive to choose working over further education. One additional issue is examined: in 1994, the government introduced a youth minimum wage for 16- to 19-year-olds – who had not been covered before – at 60% of the adult minimum. The applicability has a significantly positive effect on schooling, increasing the enrollment rate by about 10 up to 15 percentage points depending on the set of included variables. Pacheco/Cruickshank argue that the underlying reason is a reduction of labor demand for teenagers. Thus, they remain in the educational system to avoid unemployment. Nevertheless, the more the teenage minimum wage is raised, the higher are the incentives to still look for an employment (cf. ibid.). This explanation supports the queuing effect outweighing the substitution effect. Correspondingly, Hyslop/Stillmann (2007) report negative educational impacts of the youth minimum wage for 16- and 17-year-old teenagers, underlining the evidence for New Zealand (cf. Hyslop/Stillman, 2007).

Analyzing a European labor market, Rice (2010) finds negative educational effects in the United Kingdom. She estimates the individual probability of being enrolled in beyond-compulsory education using a CL model. Accounting for the fact that the UK government introduced a youth minimum wage for 18- to 21-year-olds in April 1999, the analysis follows a difference-in-difference approach: in the same school-year cohort, there are 18-year-olds under treatment of youth minimum eligibility while their 17-year-old classmates form the control group. The resulting indicator is interacted with the hourly regional wage floor relative to the corresponding mean wage. The estimation produces evidence of a negative impact on the subsequent enrollment probability in non-compulsory education (cf. Rice, 2010). Hence, higher incentives to leave school are set in regions which are affected by the minimum to a greater extent. A similar analysis is by Antòn/Muñoz de Bustillo (2011) who determine the educational effect of a stepwise raise of the Spanish youth minimum for 16- and 17-year-olds between 1995 and 1998. Using the 18- to 20-year-olds as the control group, the regression suggests that the raise of the youth minimum wage to the adult level is followed by a significant 1.6 percentage point decrease in the probability of being enrolled in formal education (cf. Antòn/Muñoz de Bustillo, 2011).

2.2.2 Evidence of Other Minimum Wage Impacts

For completeness, the small number of studies finding other than negative educational effects of minimum wages shall be presented as well. Neumark/Wascher (2003) focus on criticizing an analysis by Evans/Turner that is made reference to in several articles for the authors found no educational effect of the U.S. minimum wage, contrasting to the majority of studies (cf. Neumark/Wascher, 2003). The critique basically arises because of an inadequate choice of data – as claim Neumark/Wascher. Evans/Turner have based their study on data gathered on a number of different cutoff dates during the years observed which yield non-uniform observation periods and thus unreliable estimation results (cf. ibid.). However, since the study has not been published and cannot be considered closely, it is not further discussed.[13]

Another empirical study finding no educational effect is conducted by Campolieti et al. (2005) which is based on Canadian survey data from 1993 to 1999. The authors adapt the panel CL analysis used by Neumark/Wascher (1995a, 1995b, 2003) in order to estimate the minimum wage impact on the enrollment-employment status of 16- to 19-year-olds (cf. Campolieti et al., 2005). In contrast to Landon (1997), Campolieti et al. can hardly find any enrollment effect. There is a large negative employment effect stating that with a 10% increase in the relative minimum wage, youth employment falls by 25%. Nevertheless, the net effect on enrollment is not significantly different from zero. The authors quote as reason that there is a negative effect on the probability of being SE but a positive effect on the probability of being SNE so that the effects sum to zero.

[13] In the studies referring to the paper *Minimum wage effects in employment and school enrollment* by Evans/Turner from 1997, it is cited as a comment and/or working paper (cf. Chaplin et al., 2003; Neumark/Wascher, 2003; Pacheco/Cruickshank, 2007). Although being obviously controversial, no published version could be found.

Thus, teenagers can either afford to stay in school without a part-time job or return to school when having lost their full-time employment because of the higher wage floor (cf. ibid.).

The reader might wonder if there is any internationally comparative analysis. Neumark/Wascher account for this question in a study from 2004 which evaluates and contrasts minimum wage effects in 17 countries, all of which are members of the Organization for Economic Cooperation and Development (OECD). As a potential reason for the lack of research in this domain, the authors point out that labor market instruments and structures substantially differ among countries. Moreover, country-specific shocks, legislations or labor market policies influence minimum wage effects. Even if a regression analysis gives the same educational impact of minimum wages for two countries, the coefficients might be incomparable. While in one country, it captures a causal effect, it could be biased for another country due to omitted structural influences. Therefore, it is necessary – yet tedious – to control for specific labor market characteristics in a cross-country analysis (cf. Neumark/Wascher, 2004; Cahuc/Zylberberg, 2004, p. 716).

To do so, the authors separate the observed countries into four groups according to the intensity of active labor market policy and the level of labor standards. The classification is based on two indices by the OECD assigning larger values to countries with higher labor standards[14] and more expansive active labor market policies[15] (cf. Neumark/Wascher, 2004; Organization for Economic Cooperation and Development, 2015a,b). The evidence indicates that a raise in relative minimum wages causes young employees aged 15 to 24 to lose employment. A 10 percentage point increase in minimum wage ratios results in mostly significant 1 to 2 percentage point decreases of the youth employment-population-ratio. Nevertheless, the effect is contrary in countries with both high degrees of active labor market policy and labor standards such as Germany: the analysis predicts a 2.7 percentage

[14] For instance, a long job tenure, strict regulations of dismissals or a common use of regular employment contracts (cf. Organization for Economic Cooperation and Development, 2015b).

[15] For instance, high public expenses on labor market programmes and a large number of participants (cf. Organization for Economic Cooperation and Development, 2015a).

point increase of the youth employment rate (cf. Neumark/Wascher, 2004). Furthermore, in line with Pacheco/Cruickshank (2007), the existence of a legal youth subminimum has positive impacts. The estimated increase of youth employment rates given a 10 percentage point increase of the adult minimum ranges between 1 and 9 percentage points, though it is not always significant. Again, this result can be plausibilized referring to the substitution of workers: employers shift their demand from low-skilled adult workers to youths who can be paid a subminimum, thereby lowering production costs (cf. ibid.).

Despite only shedding light on the impact on employment, this study confirms the supposition that labor market structures and other simultaneous policy measures induce differing minimum wage effects. In further considerations, this fact should be born in mind for the necessity of a country-specific analysis is pointed out. Table A.1 in appendix A provides a resuming overview of the studies discussed, the methods used and their results. Summing up the widespread reflections on the state of research, four essential conclusions can be made:

1. The empirical evidence mostly reports negative educational effects of minimum wages. Although, both the Queuing Hypothesis and the Substitution Hypothesis can be supported, the dominance of overall negative effects suggests that educational disincentives set by higher wages tend to outweigh positive incentives set by substitution behaviour on the labor demand side.

2. Most studies rely on relative instead of absolute minimum wages to represent the degree of minimum affection. The wage floor is mostly set into relation to a region average which allows to control for regional economic characteristics (cf. Antòn/Muñoz de Bustillo, 2011; Campolieti et al., 2005; Ehrenberg/Marcus, 1982; Neumark/Wascher, 1995a,b, 2003; Rice, 2010). From a technical point of view, relative minimum wages are also useful to ensure a higher variation of values over individuals.

3. The inclusion of various control variables is recommended to avoid an omitted variable bias. Educational choices are likely to depend on personal characteristics, such as

ethnicity, gender and family background (cf. Ehrenberg/Marcus, 1982; Landon, 1997; Mincer/Leighton, 1980), as well as on socio-economic influences, e. g. the probability of being employed (cf. Currie/Fallick, 1996; Mincer/Leighton, 1980). To include personal aspects, a micro-level estimation seems preferable. Furthermore, as most influences are unchanging either over individuals or over time, a panel regression with fixed effects helps to include them, especially if difficult to measure. As could be learned from the literature review, the analysis of individual educational decisions exhibits the use of adequate regression models for discrete choices.

4. There is evidence of the fact that country-specific labor market institutions influence minimum wage effects which is meaningful for the present analysis. In Germany, one feature of that kind is the dual apprenticeship system which is used to a lesser extent in other countries (cf. Acemoglu/Pischke, 1998; Franz/Soskice, 1995). In particular, it implies a different cost structure of education since training is partly employer-financed and apprentices receive a reduced payment. Therefore, the transferabililty of the presented results to the German labor market is challenged. With regard to the empirical analysis, the working hypothesis of a non-negative educational effect of minimum wages is formulated due to an activizing labor market which promotes professional skill acquisition (cf. Acemoglu/Pischke, 1998; Franz/Soskice, 1995).

One crucial issue that is yet to address is the short period of validity of the German statutory minimum wage which is less than one year. Thus, a reliable data base to conduct an empirical analysis is not available yet. However, the following section discusses sectoral minimum wages as an alternative form and their operationality. In a second step, the new general minimum wage legislation is described. The considerations aim at providing a deeper insight into the regulations and the discussion caused by establishing youth subminima.

3 Minimum Wages in Germany

As pointed out, most empirical analyses base on minimum wages varying by regions or demographic characteristics. In Germany, another form of wage floors has been prevalent for the last decades: minimum wages on sectoral or industry level. The purpose of this section is to outline how the respective regulations are implemented and whom they affect. Moreover, their relevance for the upcoming regression analysis is explained. The considerations then lead over to the second part which observes the new country-wide minimum wage in more detail. Special emphasis is put on the discussion about youth exemptions which is linked to the research question.

3.1 Generally Binding Sectoral Minimum Wages

Considering literature on minimum wages, their widespread international establishment is clearly recognized (cf. Cahuc/Zylberberg, 2004, p. 715). Common practice is to fix a statutory wage floor on national or regional (e. g. state or province) level (cf. section 2.2). The history of German minimum wages – at least up to 2014 – is characterized by another form. Setting wage floors was not a public affair but part of a *collective bargaining agreement* (CBA), made by employers' associations and trade unions. Normally, the bargaining parties represent labor demand and supply side in the same economic sector, industry or occupational group.[16] Their right to negotiate and define labor standards is laid down by the Collective Agreement Act (CAA) while one main point is the stipulation of wage floors. In addition, the maximum amount of working hours, the minimum of holidays due or pension regulations are fixed (cf. §§ 1, 2, 5 CAA). Furthermore, specific CBAs regulate the rewards and working conditions of youth employees and apprentices

[16] The term *sector* is generally used in order to describe the scope of agreements. However, it mostly does not correspond to official statistical definitions of economic sectors.

(cf. § 5 CAA; Federal Ministry of Labor and Social Affairs, 2015b). In addition, every firm is allowed to make specific agreements concerning labor conditions as long as they are in favor of their employees and set firm level standards which are at least as high as standards set by a sectoral CBA (cf. § 4, art. 3 CAA).

Basically, CBAs only affect individuals represented by the bargaining parties, thus, workers who are members of the labor union and firms that belong to the employers' association (cf. §§ 3, 4 CAA). All other agents in the same occupational group face other – potentially lower – standards. To support workers' equality, German law entitles the MLSA to declare a CBA *generally binding* for all firms and workers in a sector. The crucial prerequiste is the predominant application of the CBA in question in its field, i. e. a considerable share of workers, which is not exactly defined (cf. § 5 CAA), is already covered by it without public intervention. The MLSA is then authorized to validate the labor standards for the non-covered workers as well (cf. § 5, art. 1, CAA). The same right is given by the Posted Workers Act (PWA) which lays down labor standards of foreign citizens working in Germany (cf. § 7, art. 1, PWA). The MLSA quarterly informs about the number of generally binding CBAs. At the moment, it lists 502 generally binding CBAs of about 70,000 CBAs in total. However, not all of them refer to wages but many are concerned with other aspects of labor standards (cf. ibid.). Recalling the research purpose, the general application of CBAs setting wage floors is of major importance: this can be considered the introduction of a sectoral minimum wage.

The first sector in which a general wage floor was established in 1997 were main construction trades. The agreement provided a minimum of 8,69 €[17] to workers in West Germany and 8,00 € to those in East Germany. Later, sectoral minimum wages have been introduced in other industries, e. g. in electrical trades, in roofing or in painting. Since the middle of the 2000s, wage floors have been in use for more service sectors, e. g. in laundry services, building cleaning, waste management, postal services and care nursing

[17] All minimum wages prior to the monetary reform in 2002 are converted to € at the official exchange rate: 1.00 DM = 0.511292 € (cf. European Council, 1998).

(cf. Boockmann et al., 2013; Federal Ministry of Labor and Social Affairs, 2015b; Frings, 2013; Rattenhuber, 2014). Table 1 shows the current levels of existing sectoral wage floors. In many cases, the level is lower in East Germany (the former German Democratic Republic). Already knowing about the meaningfulness of economic differences by regions from section 2.2, these regulations are probably the consequence of a wage floor adaption to the regional average (cf. tab. D.1).

Table 1: Current Levels of Sectoral Wage Floors in €, December 2015

Sector	West	East
Agriculture, Gardening & Forestry	7.40	7.20
Barbering	8.50	
Building Cleaning	9.55	8.50
Butchery	8.60	
Chimney Sweep Trades	12.78	
Electrical Trades	10.10	9.35
Hard Coal Mining	12.35	
Care Nursing	9.40	8.65
Main Construction Trades	11.15	10.75
Laundry Services	8.50	8.00
Professional Education	13.35	12.50
Painting & Varnishing	10.00	
Roofing	11.85	
Scaffolding	10.50	
Subcontracted Work	8.80	8.20
Textile Industry	8.50	7.50

Notes: The wage floor levels are taken from the respective official regulations in effect which can be found in the laws directory.

Sources: MLSA, minimum wage regulations; author's illustration

For several reasons, sectoral minimum wages are well operational in an empirical analysis. First, they represent an alternative, common form of wage floors in Germany that has been in use for up to 18 years. Compared to the statutory minimum wage which is not evaluable yet, this spatial and temporal spread yields a more compassing data base. With the objective of examining professional skill acquisition that usually takes several years, a cross-sectional analysis respecting only one point in time appears to be inferior to a longitudinal analysis. Second, generally binding wage floors apply to all workers in a sector with no union membership required. This aspect is crucial for observing occupational choices of youths. As school-leavers who are unlikely to belong to a labor union already, youths probably pay little attention to present or future wages of union members whereas a general minimum wage without restrictions appears to be rather influential. To clarify the incentive structure, it is pointed out that none of the regulations implies a minimum eligibility of apprentices so that a wage floor payment is only realized in case of a regular (skilled or unskilled) employment. Finally, a technical aspect conclusively remarked in section 2.2 can be taken up: sectoral minimum wages provide a larger variation among individuals than a nation-wide one. This advantage is even greater when computing relative minimum wages, e. g. on state or sector level.

A detailed presentation of the evaluation of sectoral minimum wages is beyond the scope of this thesis. Therefore, it is only mentioned briefly that empirical studies mostly found a positive impact on wages accompanied by a contractory effect on wage distributions which is in accordance with politically intended goals (cf. Boockmann et al., 2013; Möller, 2012; Rattenhuber, 2014). A decline of employment as predicted by economic theory takes place in manufacturing industries in East Germany. However, employment effects of sectoral minimum wages are mostly insignificant (cf. Boockmann et al., 2013; Frings, 2013; Möller, 2012). Attention shall be drawn to the fact that the degree of affection is again meaningful. The amount of job losses is higher in areas which are affected by wage floors to a greater extent (cf. Frings, 2013; Möller, 2012). Hence, this explains the regionally different wage floors (cf. tab. 1). To accomplish a lower degree of affection, minimum wage levels are adapted to the specific economic situation that obviously differs in West and East Germany.

According to the rising number of sectoral minimum wages in the past 15 years, a potential conclusion to arrive at is that the influence of unions and the conventionality of CBAs are growing. Looking at the evidence (cf. fig. 1), the opposite is the case: the overall presence of CBAs has been declining. While in 1998, 76% of workers in West Germany and 63% of workers in East Germany have been covered by a firm- or sector-level CBA, these shares have been decreasing to 60% and 47% respectively in 2014 (cf. Institute of Economic and Social Research, 2015). Figure 1 additionally displays the fraction of employees being members of a labor union which is also declining. This drop is tied to an increasing desire of labor flexibility: both workers and firms wish to quickly adapt to labor market shocks, technological progress or global competition which is hardly possible with fixed standards (cf. Eichhorst/Marx, 2011; Fitzenberger et al., 2011).

Figure 1: Trade Union Density and Collective Bargaining Coverage Rates in Germany, 1990-2013

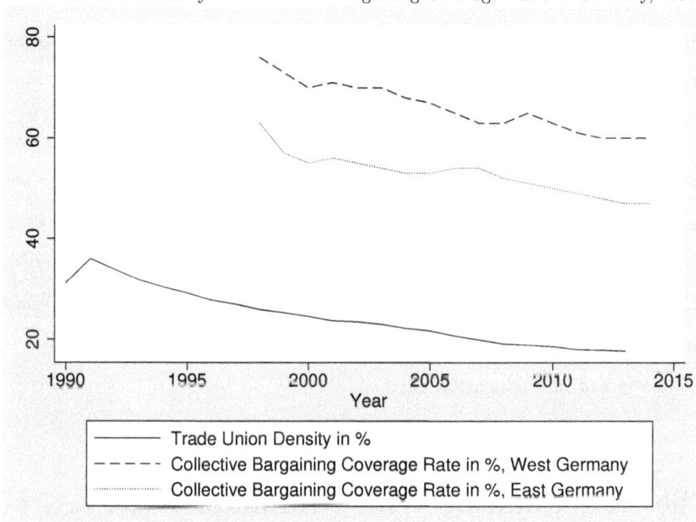

Notes: Trade Union Density: percentage share of employees being member of a trade union, *Collective Bargaining Coverage Rate:* percentage share of employees covered by a collective bargaining agreement on firm or sectoral level.

Sources: OECD, Institute of Economic and Social Research; author's figure

As unions act in favor of employees' interests, the reduction in power implies a risk of lowering labor standards and wages (cf. Antonczyk et al., 2010). Indeed, empirical evidence of rising wage inequality is observed: Dustmann et al. (2009) find that from 1990 to 2004 daily wages at the top of the distribution, i. e. the 85%-quantile, rise by

13% for men and 17% for women.[18] Over the same period, the 15%-quantile of the wage distribution did not change for women and decreased by 5% for men, thereby widening the gap between top and bottom (cf. Dustmann et al., 2009). Antonczyk et al. (2010) report similar evidence analyzing the gap between the 90%- and the 10%-quantile of the wage distribution (cf. Antonczyk et al., 2010). One potential explanation adduced by the authors is the decline in workers' representation by unions. They also mention that demand and wage premia for well-educated workers have constantly risen (cf. Antonczyk et al., 2010; Dustmann et al., 2009) which is in line with a substitution behavior of employers and the working hypothesis formulated here.

By extension, a political and media discussion about public intervention to stop labor market polarization had been launched. In particular, the introduction of a statutory minimum wage was considered a feasible countermeasure to a widening wage gap (cf. German Social Democratic Party, 2015; Möller, 2014; Müller/Steiner, 2009; German Green Party, 2013, pp. 89-90). Since 2015, the nation-wide wage floor is in effect. The legislation is presented in the following section with regard to precautions taken to avoid negative employment and education effects.

3.2 The New Country-Wide Minimum Wage

At the beginning of this thesis, the controversial and polarizing discussion about the general minimum wage in Germany has been illustrated. Despite the concerns expressed by the critics, the proponents achieved their aim of successfully confirming the regulation: MWL was officially introduced on January 1, 2015. Independent of occupation or position, every worker in Germany is now applicable to a gross hourly minimum wage of at least 8.50 € (cf. § 1 MWL). To ensure that monthly minimum payments are not offset by a

[18] Dustmann et al. (2009) only refer to full-time workers aged 21 to 60. Furthermore, they speak of considerable differences in wages between West and East Germany which prompt them to limit the analysis to West Germany (cf. Dustmann et al., 2009).

higher amount of working hours, employers are legally responsible to document both the time worked and the wages paid in their firms. Paying a subminimum wage carries financial penalties (cf. §§ 16, 17, 21 MWL).

Although the unconditional generality of the minimum wage is emphasized in the law's first paragraph (cf. § 1 MWL), it is in fact not existent. Beforehand, potentially negative effects have been investigated in a number of studies, mostly commissioned by the government or the MLSA and primarly focussing on employment effects. For a hypothetical gross hourly minimum of 7.50 €, a compression of the wage structure and growing incomes for poorer households have been predicted (cf. Bauer et al., 2009; Knaab/Schöb, 2008; Müller/Steiner, 2009). A full-time worker having earned a wage of 5.00 € so far would experience an increase of net monthly income by 32% due to the assumed wage floor (cf. Knaab/Schöb, 2008). However, this development is only said to take place for individuals remaining employed. In fact, with a statutory minimum wage of 7.50 €, a potential loss of up to 850,000 jobs, mainly part-time and marginal employment, is a conceivable scenario (cf. Bauer et al., 2009; Knaab/Schöb, 2008). Since specific subgroups such as youths or marginally employed workers are relatively more affected by a minimum due to previously lower rewards, their risk of unemployment is higher (cf. Knaab/Schöb, 2008; Müller/Steiner, 2009).

Following these statements and warnings of experts, the legislative has temporarily or permanently excepted some risk groups from the minimum. First, the minimum wage is not immediately used in all economic sectors but there is a transition period up to 2017. During these years, the application of sectoral CBAs implying subminima and stepwise increases to the general minimum is allowed (cf. § 24 MWL). This exception is used in laundry services, textile industries or subcontracted work, for example (cf. tab. 1 and minimum wage legislations). The delayed introduction is an instrument to slowly adapt to the minimum in low-wage sectors. Furthermore, former long-time unemployed persons are not eligible to the wage floor during the first six months of a new employment (cf. § 22 MWL).

With regard to youths, two exceptions are made. Under-agers without a completed professional education as well as apprentices and interns[19] are not applicable to the minimum wage (cf. § 22 MWL). The sustaining argumentation is twofold. On the one hand, it refers to the labor supply side and to the statements of the Human Capital Theory: the exception is necessary to ensure that youths are not discouraged from completing their professional education which is assumed to be the case if they were eligible for the minimum wage (cf. Amlinger et al., 2014; Federal Ministry of Labor and Social Affairs, 2015a; Möller, 2014). This is to prevent the queuing behavior of school-leavers. On the other hand, the issue of potential dismissals is addressed. If low-skilled youths were subject to the minimum wage, employers would reduce their demand for this group. Consequently, less employment for young workers, especially less apprenticeship places, would be available yielding a lower overall level of education (cf. Amlinger et al., 2014; Federal Ministry of Labor and Social Affairs, 2015a; Möller, 2014; Schulten/Horn, 2014). Thus, the exceptions serve at avoiding both negative employment and education effects at the same time. With regard to the minimum wage effects from other countries as well as to the positive experiences with youth subminima, the legislative follows the deduced political implications (cf. chapter 2.2; Amlinger et al., 2014; Möller, 2014).

Notwithstanding, critics assess the youth exception as unfair and inadequate for several reasons: primarily, workers' representants argue that the exemptions strongly contrast with the law's aim to promote equality among workers since youths are discriminated against (cf. Amlinger et al., 2014). Abstracting from any legal issues, the exceptions are unnecessary from an economic point of view either. Particularly, it is noted that underagers form a negligibly small fraction of active labor market participants (cf. Amlinger et al., 2014; Möller, 2014). The majority of youths is still enrolled in school beyond their 18th birthday. Full-aged, unskilled school-leavers instead are applicable for the minimum so that negative incentives are not offset for this group. The age limit of 18 years is regarded

[19] The exception is only valid for voluntary internships that last less than three months (cf. § 22 MWL).

as too low since it actually fails to include most school-leavers making an occupational decision (cf. Amlinger et al., 2014; Möller, 2014).

Furthermore, the substitution of low-skilled adult workers with youth employees is likely to be expanded if the latter are less costly to hire (cf. Amlinger et al., 2014; Schulten/Horn, 2014). The considerations concerning the Substitution Hypothesis in section 2.1 have shown that, despite no net employment or education effect, the group structure of employees is changed in case of a subsititution which results in a labor marginalization of dismissed adult workers (cf. Eichhorst/Marx, 2011).

As a third point, another social objection is raised: the German apprenticeship system is viewed as an ideal form of a smooth transition from school to employment, combining both practical and theoretical training at a reduced payment (cf. Büchel, 2002). It is considered the usual way for youths to enter the labor market if not pursuing an academic path. Critics argue that this well-established social norm (cf. Acemoglu/Pischke, 1998) represents a form of prevention of educational disincentives. Preferring an unskilled employment over an apprenticeship is not socially accepted and cuts future employment opportunities (cf. Amlinger et al., 2014; Büchel, 2002). Occupational decisions are assumed to depend on various personal and social factors among which minimum wages are rather subordinate (cf. Schulten/Horn, 2014, section 2.2). Finally, trade union representants instance sectoral minimum wages as yet existing incentives for unskilled work which have not been counteracted in a similar way. According to them, sectoral wage floors have not discouraged youths from undergoing professional training since school-leavers correctly determine the future benefits of skill acquisition (cf. Agell/Lommerud, 1997; Amlinger et al., 2014). However, none of the judgements can be undergirded by empirical evidence. As there is no specific study for Germany yet which examines the educational effects of minimum wages, there is no reliable knowledge of real effects (cf. Möller, 2014).

The reasonings of both the legislative and the critics illustrate the benefit to derive from the upcoming analysis. By shedding light on the actual educational effects of minimum wages, it contributes to the discussion by scientifically supporting one line of argumentation. Deductions concerning the necessity and reasonability of a youth exemption can be drawn. In the following section, the empirical framework is precisely outlined.

4 Methodological Approach

The preceeding considerations have revealed mostly negative educational effects of minimum wages. In order to determine which impact can be observed on the German labor market, the empirical approach is developped. To that end, a suitable dependent choice variable capturing the decisions of youths is constructed. Furthermore, possible exogenous influences are discussed. Based on this, an appropriate regression technique is chosen taking account of previous research. Afterwards, the data base in use is introduced.

4.1 Model Specification

4.1.1 Capture of Endogenous and Exogenous Variables

Most previous studies estimate the probability of choosing an educational or occupational activity from a set of discrete alternatives, depending on minimum wages. The sets applied consist of formal schooling and employment plus their combinations as alternatives to choose from. However, options differ for German school leavers. Making a crucial assumption, the analysis is limited to individuals who already finished formal schooling, both sucessfully and unsuccessfully. By that, the activity of further schooling to obtain a higher degree is ruled out. Individuals with no or a lower to medium secondary degree (*Hauptschule* or *Realschule* degree) are qualified for an employment but not for academic education. Thus, they are free to decide whether to enter the labor market directly as unskilled workers or to pursue a path of professional education by doing an apprenticeship. With the higher secondary degrees, *Fachabitur* or *Abitur*, individuals can enter the academic track of education as well (cf. Franz/Soskice, 1995; Riphahn, 2002). Consequently, there are two possibilities to choose from for youths without higher secondary degrees and three for those qualified for university. Only the respective vertical choice is examined, i. e. whether to become a skilled worker in a certain field. The horizontal choice of occupational fields is neglected here.

The decision of interest is the binary one between unskilled employment or professional training that individuals without (Fach-)Abitur make which is for two reasons: first, the youth exception in the MWL has been formulated to prevent discouraging educational effects regarding apprenticeship training in particular. Furthermore, the number of apprenticeship opportunities should not be reduced as a reaction to minimum wages on the employers' side (cf. Federal Ministry of Labor and Social Affairs, 2015a; section 3.2). Thus, the exemption rather refers to individuals who do not participate in academic education. As a second aspect, recall the Human Capital Theory which states that there are no negative educational incentives for higher skill groups which are unaffected by the minimum. Since academic education is the highest achievable level in Germany, expected future payments are likely to exceed legal wage floors. Therefore, the influence of minimum wages on academic education is assumed to be small (cf. Agell/Lommerud, 1997).

The educational choice can be represented in two ways with respect to the time of observation. On the one hand, the ongoing activity is captured, i. e. if an individual is receiving education at the moment. This is the specification mostly followed in the literature. On the other hand, the level of completed education can be observed. For this purpose, one measure is the *International Standard Classification of Education* (ISCED) scale which classifies primary, secondary, post-secondary (i. e. professional) and tertiary (i. e. academic) education in ascending order (cf. UNESCO Institute for Statistics, 2012, pp. 13, 25-62). It comprises of eight categories with early childhood education being the lowest possible level and doctoral education being the most advanced[20] (cf. ibid., pp. 25-62). Since the ISCED level captures the highest degree achieved, differences in education only become visible with completion of the respective activity. With regard to minimum

[20] Since the categorization is to some extent different in the dataset used later, an exact definition of levels is given then.

wages, the ongoing educational status is likely to depend on more recent minimum wage realizations than the completed level of education. In the following, the current educational activity is determined as the main outcome while the level of completed education serves as an alternative.

Section 3 has already shed light on generally binding sectoral minimum wages which are used as regressors. Beside their absolute levels, relative wage floors are computed which illustrate varying degrees of affection. Following previous studies, the so-called *Kaitz index* (cf. Cahuc/Zylberberg, 2004) is constructed. In countries with regional wage floors, it is usually computed as the ratio of a regional minimum to a regional mean or median wage. The specification is slightly different here: the Kaitz index is the sectoral minimum wage, valid for an individual i at time t, relative to the respective federal state median wage:

$$Kaitz_{it} = \frac{SectoralMinWage_{it}}{median(StateWage_{it})} \tag{8}$$

Since minimum wages are adapted to West and East Germany (cf. section 3.1, tab. 1), it seems reasonable to set the sectoral wage floors into relation to the state median, thereby taking economic aspects on an even lower level into account. Moreover, with respect to the occupational groups eligible for minimum wages, too few observations or a homogenous wage structure lead to unreliable occupational means. Thus, the spatial adaption is preferred. However, the regression analysis will be carried out using both absolute and relative minimum wages. A considerable point is that wages typically follow a stochastic or deterministic trend. Using non-stationary regressors is likely to bias estimates or detect only spurious relations (cf. Greene, 2012, pp. 985-986). Consequently, the wage series will be tested for trends first and corrected if necessary.

In addition to the wage minima, several control variables are included in order to respect the complexity and diversity of occupational choices, see section 2.2. Furthermore, the liability to an omitted variable bias is reduced and the consistency of estimators is improved (cf. Greene, 2012, p. 97). The control variables considered can be separated into two subgroups.

To begin with, the educational decision depends on an individual's personal characteristics. Common control variables are gender and nationality reflecting that choices differ according to distinct preferences, social norms or discrimination (cf. Büchel, 2002; Campolieti et al., 2005; Constant/Zimmermann, 2003; Landon, 1997). Furthermore, the school degree obtained prior to the decision might have an impact: the access to certain activities or jobs is refused with lower degrees. Employers may moreover take higher qualifications as a sign of higher productivity or apitude (cf. Cahuc/Zylberberg, 2004, pp. 80-83; Agell/Lommerud, 1997).

The second group of controls is formed by socio-economic variables. In particular, studies have provided evidence of the importance of parents' income and education when it comes to professional careers. Reflecting an educational preference, parents are likely to pursue a children's level of education similar to their own (cf. Checchi, 2006, pp. 116, 216-219; Constant/Zimmermann, 2003; Dustmann, 2004; Modesto, 2003). Beyond that, it has been mentioned that parental income is an educational determinant as wealthier families are able to financially support further training (cf. Checchi, 2006, pp. 29-30; section 2.1).[21]

To model a competitive situation on the labor market or in the educational system, the size of the youth cohort, relative to the total population, is taken account of (cf. Riphahn, 2002). A second measure is given by the number of apprenticeship places which represents the demand for youth workers and the opportunities to receive professional education. Building on this, unemployment rates serve as another control. By illustrating current

21 To compensate for this inequality, young people in Germany can receive public support during educational activities provided by individual transfer payments according to the Federal Training Assistence Act (cf. Riphahn, 2002). As these transfers are calculated based on parental income and tied to an ongoing educational activity, there appears to be an endogeneity problem so that they are not considered here.

employment prospects, they indicate the overall economic situation which encourages or discourages youths to undergo further education (cf. Büchel, 2002; Mincer/Leighton, 1980; Riphahn, 2002). For the socio-economic influences, the stationarity of variables must be checked as well.

Furthermore, it is questionable if minimum wage levels really have an impact on concurrent educational activities. For example, application processes take a certain amount of time and apprenticeships usually cannot be started directly. Therefore, it appears helpful to use lagged values of influential variables (cf. Neumark/Wascher, 1995a,b). Doing so also addresses potential endogeneity issues: occupational activities and wages captured at the same time may depend on one another. For the number of apprenticeship places and the probability of being an apprentice, the causality can as well run in both directions. With lagged values of one variable, this interdependence is ruled out to a certain extent. The regular duration of an apprenticeship is three years (cf. § 5, art. 1 VTA). Hence, the maximum lag of wage floors is a three-period one. For time-variant controls, at least one-period lagged values are included.

4.1.2 Regression Models

Since the dependent choice variable is binary, it is properly estimated using a logit model. Many previous studies modelling a discrete choice from two or more alternatives apply a CL model (cf. Campolieti et al., 2005; Neumark/Wascher, 1995a,b). It yields the individual probability of choosing one alternative n relative to the total set of J alternatives (cf. Wooldridge, 2010, pp. 497-499). For the binary choice here, the CL model equals a panel logit approach including individual-fixed effects α_i which represent unobserved time-constant educational influences, such as intelligence or talents, but also the mentioned time-invariant individual characteristics X_i (cf. Allison, 2009, pp. 29-33), e. g. sex, ethnicity or school qualifications which have been shown to be educational determinants (cf. Ehrenberg/Marcus, 1982; Landon, 1997; section 2.2.1). As they do not change over time, coefficients on these characteristics are not reported in most cases (cf. Allison, 2009, p. 29). Furthermore, the model allows to control for the mentioned time-variant influences Z_t consisting of unemployment rates, the number of apprenticeship places and the relative youth cohort size. Modelling the choice depending on both Kaitz indices and other characteristics, the following panel CL model including time effects λ_t is estimated (cf. Greene, 2012, p. 762):

$$P(Y_{it} = 1|\alpha_i, \sum_{k=0}^{3} Kaitz_{it-k}, X_i, Z_t, \lambda_t) = \frac{exp(\alpha_i + \sum_{k=0}^{3} \beta_k Kaitz_{it-k} + \gamma X_i + \delta Z_t + \lambda_t)}{1 + exp(\alpha_i + \sum_{k=0}^{3} \beta_k Kaitz_{it-k} + \gamma X_i + \delta Z_t + \lambda_t)} \quad (9)$$

However, a crucial model demand must be fulfilled. A CL model is only estimated consistently if the assumption of independence of irrelevant alternatives (IIA) is met (cf. Borooah, 2002, pp. 72-74). The IIA expresses that the probability ratio of a choice between two alternatives A or B is constant regardless of any other alternatives included in the choice set (cf. Greene, 2012, p. 807; Hensher/Greene, 2003). In the present case, an individual's relative probability of choosing an apprenticeship instead of an unskilled employment should be unchanged if academic education was included as a third possibility. This strict assumption is not discussed in earlier studies which apply a CL model (Campolieti et al., 2005; Ehrenberg/Marcus, 1982; Neumark/Wascher, 1995a,b, 2003). One can argue that, since they all limit their samples to teenagers with a maximum age of 19, they do not face other alternatives than schooling or working: from the cited studies, we can assume that either teenagers work part-time or they work full-time without having graduated from high school so that their access to the academic track is refused. Thus, the full set of options is displayed and there are no other potentially disturbing alternatives left out. However, the assumption might still be violated as we talk about the dependence on *irrelevant* alternatives. Thus, although the youth sample considered is not qualified for university, their choice may nevertheless depend on this possibility. Another method used in the previous literature to avoid a violation of the IIA assumption is to rely on a macro-level dependent variable such as enrollment rates which is estimated without using a CL approach (cf. Chaplin et al., 2003; Hyslop/Stillman, 2007; Landon, 1997; Pacheco/Cruickshank, 2007). However, a great disadvantage arises when it comes to the inclusion of personal characteristics which is complicated with a non-individual dependent variable. Consequently, both modifying the regression to avoid a logit model and the unreliability of results due to violated assumptions are undesirable.

Therefore, a *mixed logit* (MIL) model is applied which allows for random variation at a specified level, e. g. for every individual. Instead of producing the same regression coefficients for all observations, it computes specific ones accounting for individual features and choice patterns (cf. Rabe-Hesketh/Skrondal, 2005, pp. 116-117; Revelt/Train, 1998). However, as the evaluation of person-specific coefficients is unpractical for large samples, the random variation is captured by an individual intercept[22] which absorbs the person-specific influences (cf. Hensher/Greene, 2003; Greene, 2012, pp. 811-812). Thus, the estimation results consist of average coefficients on the regressors, comparable to the CL model, and the standard deviation of person-specific intercepts. Since the latter are allowed to be heteroskedastic and serially correlated, the model not only addresses a violation of IIA but also other issues regarding correlation of the error terms ϵ_{it} which are identically and independently distributed afterwards (cf. Hensher/Greene, 2003). Hence, if the CL assumptions are violated, the MIL model produces more reliable results. For the present purpose, the apprenticeship probability P_{it} can be stated as follows (cf. Hensher/Greene, 2003; Revelt/Train, 1998):

$$P_{it} = \int L_{it} f(\eta|\Omega) d\eta \tag{10}$$

with the likelihood function

22 The person-specific intercept can be understood as the sum of deviations of the person-specific estimates from the average estimates multiplied with the individual set of exogenous regressors (cf. Revelt/Train, 1998).

$$L_{it}(\eta) = \frac{exp(\alpha + \sum_{k=0}^{3} \beta_k \Delta Kaitz_{it-k} + \gamma X_i + \delta \Delta Z_t + \lambda_t + \eta_{it})}{1 + exp(\alpha + \sum_{k=0}^{3} \beta_k \Delta Kaitz_{it-k} + \gamma X_i + \delta \Delta Z_t + \lambda_t + \eta_{it})} \quad (11)$$

and $f(\eta|\Omega)$ being the density function of the random intercept η (cf. Hensher/Greene, 2003; Greene, 2012, pp. 811-812). Instead of the relative minimum wage, the regression equations can be formulated with an absolute minimum wage MW_{it} analogously. Furthermore, since the ISCED levels imply a rank order, an *ordered logit* (OL) model is estimated in this alternative case, ideally also including FE (cf. Baetschmann et al., 2015). In addition, a linear probability model is run as a basic approach.

Having discussed the model specification, the actual data base is now explained. Background information on the sources and the survey methods are given. Moreover, descriptive statistics and stylized facts allow to familiarize with the dataset and point at considerable findings.

4.2 Data Base

4.2.1 Data Base Description

The dataset used combines information from three different sources. The main are micro-level data taken from the German household panel GSOEP which is an annual survey realized by the German Institute for Economic Research (DIW) in Berlin. All members aged 16 or older living in one household are interviewed about subjects of daily life, such as occupation, income and spendings, family and friends, living conditions, health, education and leisure activities (cf. Frick/Haisken-DeNew, 2005, pp. 16-17, 21). The survey is representative; information is gathered on more than 20,000 respondents (cf. ibid., p. 26). The latest available version covers a time period of 30 years from 1984 up to 2013. The GSOEP is composed of several samples: while at the beginning of the survey, only inhabitants of the Federal Republic of Germany could be interviewed, samples for individuals in the former German Democratic Republic were added after the reunification in 1990. Furthermore, stepwise extensions have been made representing special groups, e. g. very wealthy persons or migrants (cf. ibid., pp. 19-20).

The GSOEP is chosen as the main data base as it provides a great amount of individual information from different fields in life. Referring to the required information described in section 4.1, it is obvious that both occupation- and work life-related characteristics are needed as well as personal information on an individual. Furthermore, the GSOEP is a longitudinal survey covering an observation period of three decades. Hence, a panel analysis involving the mentioned advantages can be conducted.

Nevertheless, additional information is used. Sectoral minimum wages are not included in the GSOEP for what reason the official legislations laying down general wage floors serve as a second source.[23] For other macro-level characteristics such as unemployment rates and apprenticeship places, data provided by the Federal Statistical Office (FSO) is used.

The overall dataset consists of 2,090,211 observations. Table 2 displays the descriptive statistics for the subsample used in the baseline regression (without controls) consisting of 8,062 observations covering the years 1994 to 2013.[24] To keep legibility, only short explanations concerning construction and coding of the variables are made here. A detailed codebook can be found in appendix B.1.[25]

Table 2: Summary Statistics, Baseline Regression Sample

Variable	Obs	Mean	Std. Dev.	Min	Max
Survey Year	8,062	2002.703	5.546	1994	2013
Educational Status	8,062	0.812	0.391	0	1
in Minimum Wage Groups	1,937	0.807	0.394	0	1
in Other Occupational Groups	6,125	0.813	0.390	0	1

23 See Laws Directory.

24 For the descriptives of the full sample and of supportive variables, see tables B.1 and B.2.

25 For further information on the variables used, consider also the GSOEP codebooks directly provided by the DIW (cf. Goebel, 2014a,b,c).

Table 2: Summary Statistics, Baseline Regression Sample - Continued

Variable	Obs	Mean	Std. Dev.	Min	Max
ISCED Level (Modified)	8,042	2.064	0.478	1	5
Minimum Wage	8,062	0.942	2.779	0	11.2
State Median Wage	8,062	13.823	2.362	8.05	19.481
Kaitz Index	8,062	0.068	0.201	0	0.904
Existence of Minimum Wage	8,062	0.104	0.306	0	1
Δ Minimum Wage	8,062	0.478	2.347	-11.05	11.2
Δ State Median Wage	7,054	0.287	0.566	-3.902	7.445
Δ Kaitz Index	8,062	0.034	0.169	-0.83	0.904
Sex	8,062	0.433	0.495	0	1
Nationality	7,148	0.126	0.332	0	1
Age	8,062	20.183	1.93	17	24
Age Group	8,062	1	0	1	1
Lower to Medium Secondary School Degree	8,062	1.558	0.588	0	2
Indicator of Higher Secondary School Degree	8,062	0	0	0	0
Required Education for Occupation	6,719	4.341569	1.189608	1	6
Federal State of Residence	8,062	8.394	3.986	1	16
State Unemployment Rate	8,062	10.997	4.706	4.2	22.1
Number of Apprenticeship Places (in Thousand)	6,771	449.091	50.539	360.016	519.554
Relative Youth Cohort Size	8,062	3.591	0.774	2.364	4.676
Monthly Post-Government Household Income (in Thousand €)	8,062	3.014	1.903	0	48.632
Δ National Unemployment Rate	8,062	-0.061	0.844	-1.9	1.3
Δ State Unemployment Rate	7,054	-0.041	1.2	-13.1	11.7
Δ Number of Apprenticeship Places	6,364	-1.042	31.253	-37.764	93.848
Δ Relative Youth Cohort Size	8,062	0.176	0.514	-0.286	1.55
Δ Household Income	7,054	0.085	1.119	-16.558	24.336
Time	8,062	2002.703	5.546	1994	2013
Economic Sector According to NACE	7,516	54.16	23.782	1	100

Sources: GSOEP, FSO, minimum wage regulations; author's calculations

A never-changing and non-transferable person number uniquely identifies the individuals. It is reused in every subsequent survey. The variable `year` gives the year under observation. Since the data before 1990 only consist of West German respondents and the first sectoral minimum wages were introduced in 1997 (see minimum wage regulations), the analysis is limited to the years 1994 to 2013. This way, the entire German population is included. The sample of youths consists of 17- to 24-year-olds which can be seen by the values of `age`.[26] Hereby, the analysis is extended to full-aged labor market entrants like it has been suggested by previous remarks (cf. Neumark/Wascher, 2010, p. 191; Pacheco/Cruickshank, 2007).

As outlined above, the main question to answer is whether a wage floor has an influence on the choice between unskilled employment or apprenticeship training. For the baseline regression model, the dependent variable `educ_stat_youth` is constructed capturing the educational status of youths. The indicator variable takes up the value 1 if an individual is doing an apprenticeship in the year under observation and the value 0 if an individual is an unskilled active worker. The variable excludes all kinds of students, either at schools or universities. They are not available on the labor market and have made an educational choice not analyzed here. Furthermore, persons doing a military/civil service are excluded as these are not considered voluntary choices. The variable takes up an average of 0.812. Thus, the fraction of apprentices is about four times higher than the fraction of unskilled workers.

For further sensitivity analyses, the variable `isced` is used which provides information on the educational attainment according to the ISCED scale. For GSOEP purposes, the levels are redefined: a value of 0 refers to individuals still attending school while level 1 refers to those with no approved schooling and level 2 to those with general secondary education. The levels 3, 4 and 5 all capture forms of post-secondary education: level 3 comprises of persons with basic vocational firm-training, level 4 of individuals with vo-

26 The lower boundary is partly imposed by the GSOEP survey method which interviews persons from the age of 16 on (cf. Frick/Haisken-DeNew, 2005, p. 21).

cational education received at specialized professional schools and level 5 of those with higher vocational education, e. g. foremen or crafts masters. Any kind of academic education is subsumed by level 6 (cf. Goebel, 2014b, p. 76). Based on this, a modified version `isced_alt` is constructed excluding students and the academic level. For the group of 17- to 24-year-olds, the variable mean is 2.06. Thus, on average, all individuals have obtained an educational level slightly higher than general schooling.

As the main regressor, sectoral mimimum wages are used (`minwage_stat`). The wage floor levels taken from the respective legislations are imputed by the following procedure: the professions subject to a generally binding minimum wage which are listed in the legislations are compared with occupational codes following the FSO-1992-classification of occupations (`occup_klas`) in the GSOEP (cf. ibid., pp. 9336-9383; Federal Statistical Office, 1992). If an individual has stated to carry out a profession with a minimum wage in use, the respective level on January 1 of the year under observation is associated.[27] The baseline regression covers a time period during which minimum wages have been valid for building cleaning, care nursing, electrical trades, hard coal mining, main construction trades, laundry services, painting & varnishing, postal services, professional education, security services and waste management.[28] For all other professions, the minimum wage is zero[29]. To clearly assign minimum wages that vary over regions, the respective indicator (`region`) or the federal state of living (`fed_state`) is taken into account. As no other information is available, it is assumed that individuals work in the state where they live. The baseline sample neglects individuals without occupational information since they cannot precisely be assigned a minimum wage.

27 One exception has been made. In January 2013, there was a minimum wage break of four weeks in waste management since the previous generally binding CBA expired by the end of 2012 while the next had been in effect from February on. However, as the non-existence of a sectoral minimum was very short, the new wage floor is treated as if having been valid for the entire year 2013 which seems reasonable, see Boockmann et al. (2013).

28 The sectoral minimum wage in roofing was introduced in 1997 (see minimum wage regulations). However, for unknown reasons, the GSOEP contains no observations for roofers according to the occupational codes.

29 For the exact list of occupation codings, see tab. B.4.

To generate the Kaitz indices, a median wage level is required. GSOEP information on gross monthly wages is combined with the individual working hours per week (work_time) to receive the gross hourly wage (wage_gro).[30] The median wage level for each federal state and year is captured by medianw_state. The ratio of the individual minimum wage to the state median is the Kaitz index kaitz_stat_reg. Both the absolute and the relative minimum wage have low mean values near 0, indicating that the fraction of individuals working in the respective sectors is relatively small. To complete the set of independent minimum variables, an indicator variable mw_exist is included coding the existence of a generally binding minimum wage as 1 and the non-existence as 0. It displays a fraction of workers in minimum wage sectors of about 10%.

The control variables discussed in section 4.1.2 are represented as follows: the personal characteristics include sex (sex) and nationality (natio) where a value of 1 represents females and non-Germans respectively. The indicator abi gives information on whether a person has obtained a higher secondary degree and is allowed to enter the academic track. As can be seen in table 2, the variable takes up the value 0 for all observations in the baseline sample since the choice of youths without higher secondary degrees is analyzed only (see section 4.1.1). In line with that, the information on school degrees (schooldeg_sec) is limited to having no, a lower (Hauptschule) or a medium (Realschule) secondary degree. The variable educ_necessary gives the required level of education to carry out an individual's current occupation. A value of 1 corresponds to no need for specific skills whereas a value of 6 stands for the requirement of academic education.

Unfortunately, the GSOEP provides only few information on parental education. Although a corresponding variable exists, the number of respondents is small and not useful for the regression analysis. To nevertheless express a young person's ability to rely on family income, the variable hh_income is included. It represents the monthly average of the annual post-government income referring to the household the individual lives in.

[30] The calculation refers to the wages of all workers to represent the actual wage structure of active labor market participants.

Thus, for the variable to fulfill its purpose, youths need to still live with their parents which cannot be proved by corresponding information. As there is no measure which appears more appropriate, the variable is used for a robustness analysis only. However, the coefficients shall be interpreted with caution.

The number of apprenticeship places is taken from FSO data (`appren_place`). It gives the total amount of places in thousands, either occupied or not, on September 1 of a year. This information is a proxy for the extent to which firms offer professional training. As apprenticeships normally start on August 1 of a year, the number on September 1 is likely to cover all places, even if offered last-minute. Since non-occupied places are reported as well, a strong endogeneity with respect to the apprenticeship decision is ruled out. As information is only available from 1998 to 2013, the observation period is slightly shortened by this control variable. The relative size of the youth cohort (`cohortsize`) is computed as the percentage share of 17- to 24-year-olds of total respondents for each year. The general economic situation is represented by the state unemployment rate in percent of civil employees (`uer_reg`). The series display the official rates according to the Federal Employment Agency. As the state unemployment rates are highly correlated with the national unemployment rate – the correlation adds up to nearly 0.9 – but as they provide more variation among observations, they are preferred. Including both national and state rates biases the estimation due to a high collinearity.[31]

Finally, time and sector effects are included as factor variables (cf. Chaplin et al., 2003; Neumark/Wascher, 1995a,b, 2003). The variable `time` represents year effects such as general changes in labor market structures that affect all individuals. Occasionally, they cannot be included. In particular, difficulties occur when examining smaller subsamples or with control variables that reflect time effects to a certain extent. The economic sector `sector_nace` completes the set of control variables. As described above, indicators of single minimum wage groups can easily be constructed by means of the respective

31 With state unemployment rates, eqs. (9) and (11) change slightly because unemployment rates do not only vary over time but also over individuals.

occupations. Unfortunately, the group of unaffected sectors cannot be separated according to similar criteria. However, including all other occupations as one homogenous group is likely to cause a misspecification. To solve this problem, the economic sector of working according to the *Nomenclature statistique des activités économiques dans la Communauté européenne* (NACE) is used (cf. European Council, 2006). This official classification by the European Union (EU) yields a differenciation within occupations without minimum wages as well. However, the sectors defined do not exactly match the minimum wage groups.

For earlier stated reasons, variables are lagged. The maximum lag of wage floor variables is a three-period one. For all time-variant controls, one-period lagged values are uniformly included.[32]

4.2.2 Stylized Facts

Figure 2 provides a closer look at the educational status and the modified ISCED level of youths in the baseline sample. It must be born in mind that the observations for the educational status are not equally distributed in the baseline sample (cf. fig. 2a). While, unfortunately, no observations are available for professional education and hard coal mining, there are more than 600 for main construction trades and more than 400 for electrical trades. In figure 2b, the development of dependent variables over time is shown. Apparently, the mean of the educational status has almost stayed constant over the years. While in 1994, the mean was at 0.655, in 2004, it had risen to 0.753 to fall again and take up a value of 0.633 in 2013. The educational preference clearly exceeds a value of 0.5. The modified ISCED level of completed education is also stable at a value slightly exceeding 2. Remember that the academic level of education is excluded here. Thus, on average, youths have obtained a school degree and some have already finished further education.

32 The analysis of longer and multiple lags has shown no considerable differences in estimates.

Figure 2: Distribution of Education, Baseline Regression Sample, 1994-2013

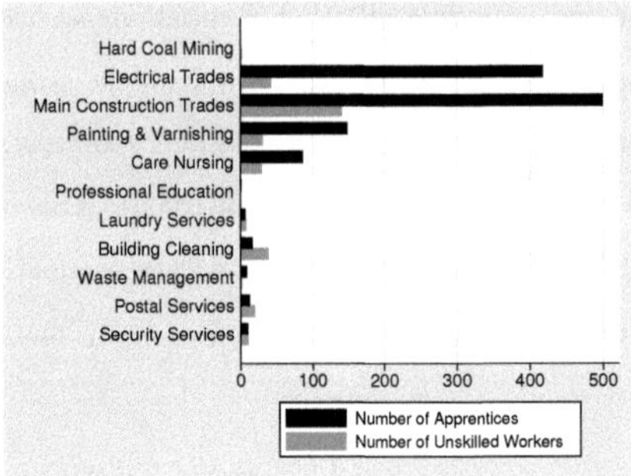

(a) Number of Observations by Minimum Wage Groups

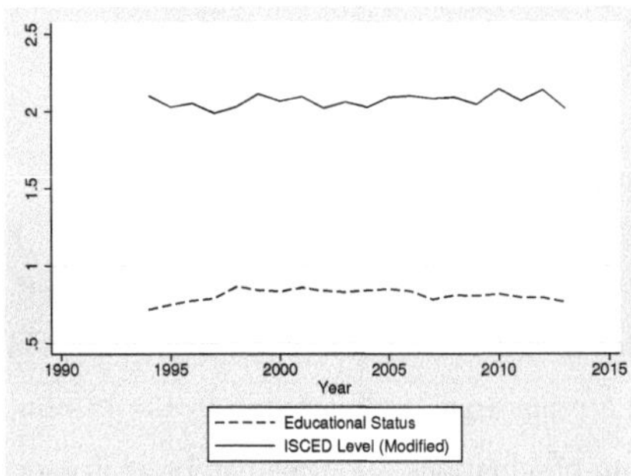

(b) Mean of Dependent Variables

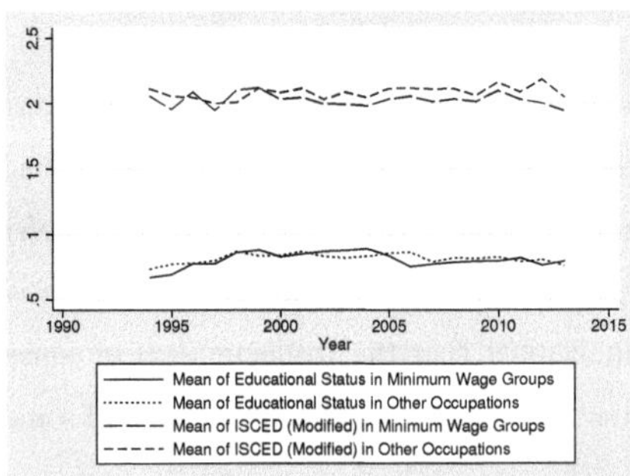

(c) Mean of Dependent Variables over Occupations

Sources: GSOEP, FSO, minimum wage regulations; author's figure

Figure 2c displays the mean values of dependent variables distinguishing between minimum wage sectors and those without a regulation. For both variables, the time lines are close to each other. Looking at the educational status in particular, the lines are almost congruent. No clear difference according to the existence of sectoral minima can be determined. The mean educational disposition seems to be the same in minimum wage groups and other occupations.

Notwithstanding, an educational development can be observed looking at the overall dataset. As displayed in figure 3a, when including the adult population and the academic tracks, the mean ISCED level increases over time, both in minimum wage groups and other sectors. In the former, the mean qualification level falls behind which explains lower wages and the resulting fixation of wage floors.

Considering figure 3b, it seems contradictory that the mean ISCED level of youths decreases over the same period. However, the observations can be interpreted consistently. First, it is necessary to include both the older population and the academic level to see an increase of education over time. This fact indicates that there has been an educational shift towards the academic level. This is in line with the rising fraction of youths that obtain a higher secondary degree, visualized by the red line in figure 3b. The falling ISCED level for youths can be explained by a larger number of school-leavers with a secondary degree, thus ISCED level 2 or 3, who remain there until the end of vocational training or university studies which might only be after their 24th birthday. Thereby, when finally achieving a higher level of education, they are not in the youth sample anymore.

These findings are crucial for the discussion. For one thing, they confirm a stronger preference for higher education which is likely to not depend on minimum wages. Second, they underline the statement that an exemption should also apply to full-aged youths since professional education is still in progress.

Figure 3: Overall Development of Education, 1990-2013

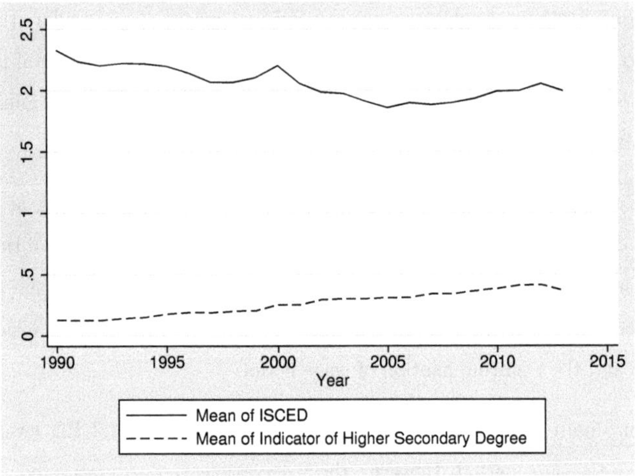

(a) Youth Aged 17-24

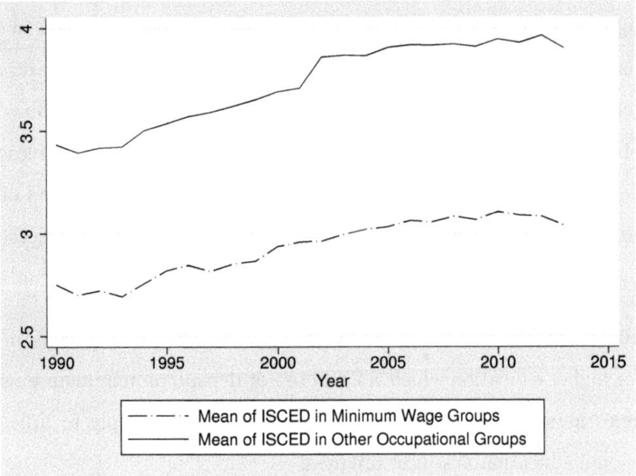

(b) Full Dataset

Sources: GSOEP, FSO, minimum wage regulations; author's figure

The preceeding considerations already brought up the problem of non-stationary wages. Figure 4 illustrates that minimum and state median wages apparently follow a rising time trend. Therefore, the stationarity over time is analyzed by a Dickey-Fuller test which indicates that the null hypothesis of a unit root cannot be rejected in nearly all cases: the variables are instationary and exhibit a stochastic trend. As this fact substantially distorts the regression results (cf. Greene, 2012, pp. 985-986), the first difference, i.e. $Y_{it} - Y_{it-1}$, for every affected variable Y_{it} is computed.

Figure 4: Minimum Wages and State Median Wages, 1990-2013

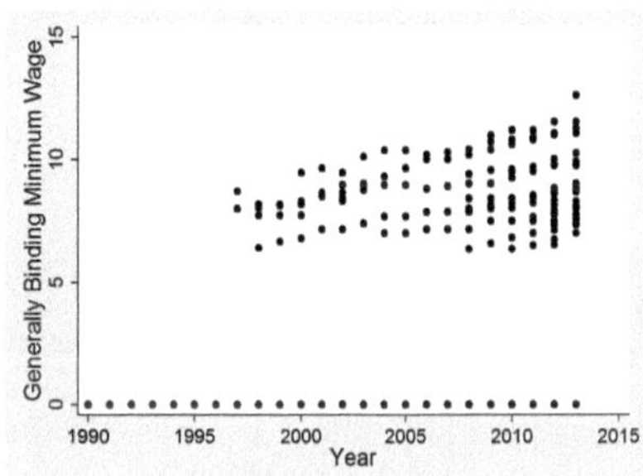

(a) Minimum Wage

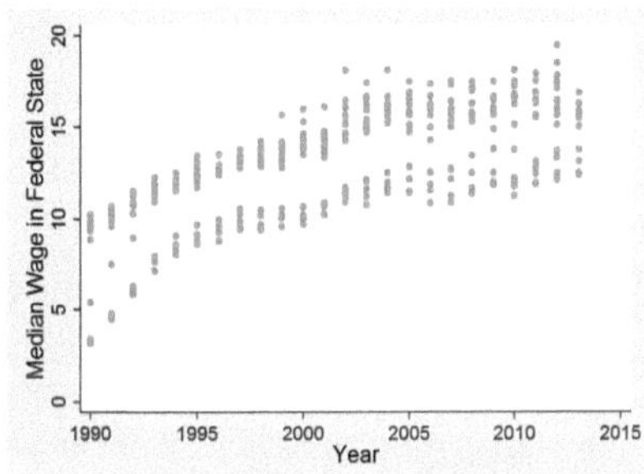

(b) State Median Wage

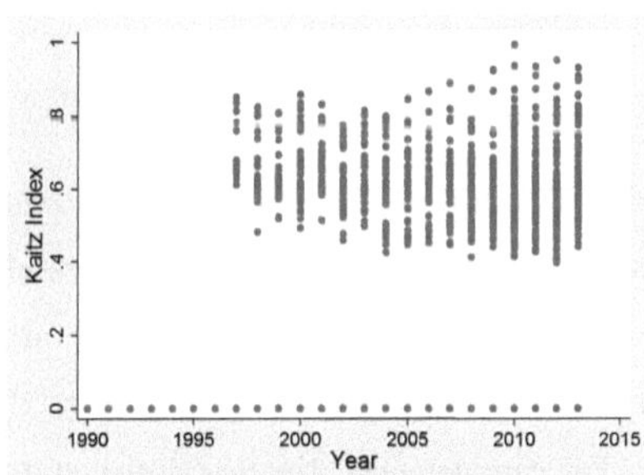

(c) Kaitz Index

Sources: GSOEP, FSO, minimum wage regulations; author's figure

Figure 5: Minimum Wages and State Median Wages, First Differences, 1991-2013

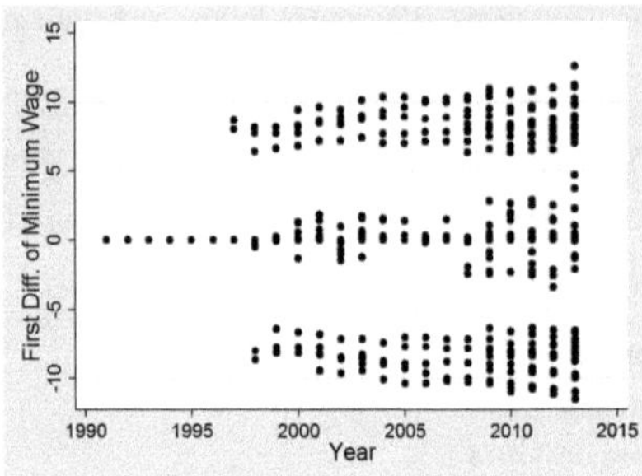

(a) Δ Minimum Wage

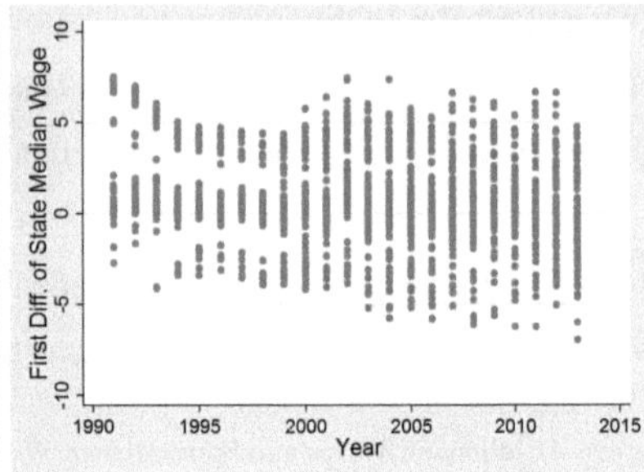

(b) Δ Median Wage

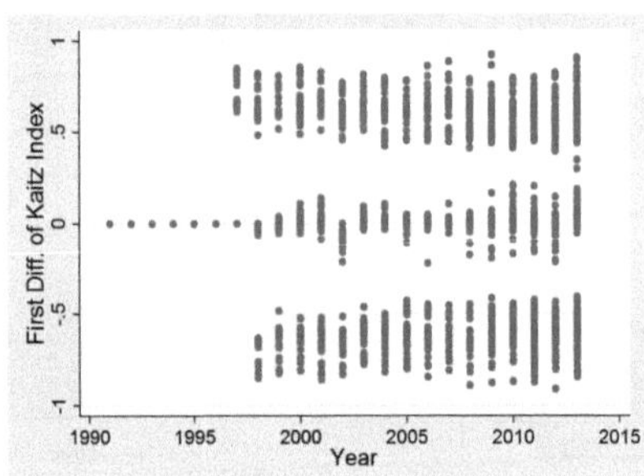

(c) Δ Kaitz Index

Sources: GSOEP, FSO, minimum wage regulations; author's figure

Figure 5 depicts the first differences of minimum and state median wages. Compared to their initial values, no trend is apparent anymore. The test results further confirm that the transformed series are stationary.[33] Since the variables capturing state unemployment rates and apprenticeship places also suffer from instationarity, their first differences are also used as regressors.[34] For completeness, the descriptive statistics of first differences

33 See tables B.5 and B.6 for the results of the Dickey-Fuller tests.

34 For the Kaitz indices and the household income, no stationarity tests are conductable. First, these variables are person-specific. Thus, there is no common time series to be tested. Second, the number of survey years varies over individuals and, in case of a very limited number, no trend can be computed. Therefore, the first differences are used to obtain a certain uniformity and stationarity is assumed. Considering fig. 5c, this seems to be adequate, at least for the Kaitz index which is the ratio of minimum wages to median wages that are mostly stationary after the transformation.

have already been presented in table 2. Computing them to achieve stationarity is preferred over applying logarithmic values since a zero minimum wage is common in the dataset. The logarithm of 0 is undefined and would yield missing values for all observations with a zero minimum wage which is undesirable. It shall not be left unsaid that, even after taking first differences, the test fails to reject the null hypothesis of instationarity of median wages in four states: North-Rhine-Westfalia, Saarland, Brandenburg and Mecklenburg-Vorpommern. Nevertheless, these states are not excluded in order to not reduce the sample size.[35]

With the analysis in view, the use of differences slightly changes the examined question: instead of estimating the effect of a minimum wage in $t-k; k = 0, 1, 2, 3$ on the educational decision in t, the respective effect of a minimum wage change from $t-k-1$ to $t-k$ is analyzed.

Having observed that the educational decision facing wage floors is stable over time, a causal relation is yet to detect. Table 3 displays the correlation matrix of variables used in the baseline regression model (plus additional control variables). The educational status is slightly positively correlated with relative minimum wage differences. For the three-period lagged minimum difference, the correlation with the educational status is negative and comparably small. The decision to include lagged values is confirmed by higher correlations of the educational status with one- and two-period lagged than with concurrent differences. High correlations can be observed for educational measures (including school degrees) and household income. Recalling the remarks made by the Human Capital Theory, the evidence supports the close relation between these quantities. The school degree obtained is also positively correlated with the educational status. This is either due to a stronger preference for further skill acquisition or a larger apprenticeship employability with a higher school qualification (cf. Agell/Lommerud, 1997; Mincer/Leighton, 1980). Another interesting finding is the strongly positive correlation of required education and

[35] As mentioned above, first differences of the Kaitz index are assumed to be stationary. A robustness check will later show whether the results differ when dropping the affected states.

Table 3: Cross-Correlation Table 1

Variables	(1)	(2)	(3)	(4)	(5)	(6)	(7)	(8)	(9)	(10)	(11)	(12)	(13)	(14)	(15)	(16)
Educational Status (1)	1.000															
(Δ Kaitz Index_t (2)	0.022	1.000														
(Δ Kaitz $\text{Index})_{t-1}$ (3)	0.052	-0.148	1.000													
(Δ Kaitz $\text{Index})_{t-2}$ (4)	0.027	-0.066	-0.174	1.000												
(Δ Kaitz $\text{Index})_{t-3}$ (5)	-0.020	-0.024	-0.057	-0.180	1.000											
Sex (6)	-0.019	-0.099	-0.083	-0.062	-0.029	1.000										
Nationality (7)	-0.156	-0.013	-0.030	-0.024	0.006	-0.013	1.000									
Lower to Medium Secondary School Degree (8)	0.169	-0.024	0.007	0.008	-0.003	0.097	-0.157	1.000								
Age (9)	-0.425	-0.085	-0.041	0.003	0.025	0.014	0.096	-0.030	1.000							
Δ State Unemployment Rate (10)	-0.025	-0.027	-0.022	-0.017	-0.007	0.001	0.020	-0.084	-0.019	1.000						
Δ Household Income (11)	0.030	0.009	0.011	0.017	-0.009	-0.037	-0.015	0.006	-0.058	0.025	1.000					
Δ Number of Apprenticeship Places (12)	-0.021	-0.004	0.041	-0.021	0.008	-0.010	-0.001	0.012	0.062	-0.149	0.009	1.000				
Δ Relative Youth Cohort Size (13)	0.035	-0.031	0.089	-0.007	0.013	0.007	0.020	0.010	-0.036	-0.180	0.002	0.146	1.000			
Required Education for Occupation (14)	0.481	-0.008	0.016	0.033	0.023	-0.034	-0.137	0.140	-0.135	-0.032	0.022	-0.021	0.046	1.000		
Time (15)	0.013	0.080	0.037	0.041	0.022	-0.014	-0.103	0.139	0.106	-0.364	-0.007	0.262	-0.100	0.047	1.000	
Economic Sector according to NACE (16)	0.012	-0.030	-0.028	-0.035	-0.029	0.371	-0.022	0.067	0.061	0.024	-0.047	0.014	-0.012	-0.016	0.003	1.000

Sources: GSOEP, FSO, minimum wage regulations; author's calculations

the educational status which points at a guidance of youths by the necessary skill level for their preferred occupation. Non-Germans are likelier to be low-skilled compared to Germans (cf. Ehrenberg/Marcus, 1982; Mincer/Leighton, 1980) whereas the difference between sexes is rather small. The role of socio-economic influences, such as unemployment rates, is still unclear as correlations are low.

The relation of Kaitz differences and the educational status is further visualized by a scatterplot in figure 6. For the one- and two-period lagged minimum wages, a small positive link is suggested: higher values of relative minimum wage differences tendencially seem to go along with higher values of the dependent variable. This graphical inspection again indicates no evidently strong relation between minimum wages and education. The regression analysis now serves to analytically determine the exact influence.

Figure 6: Scatterplot of Educational Status against Relative Minimum Wage Differences

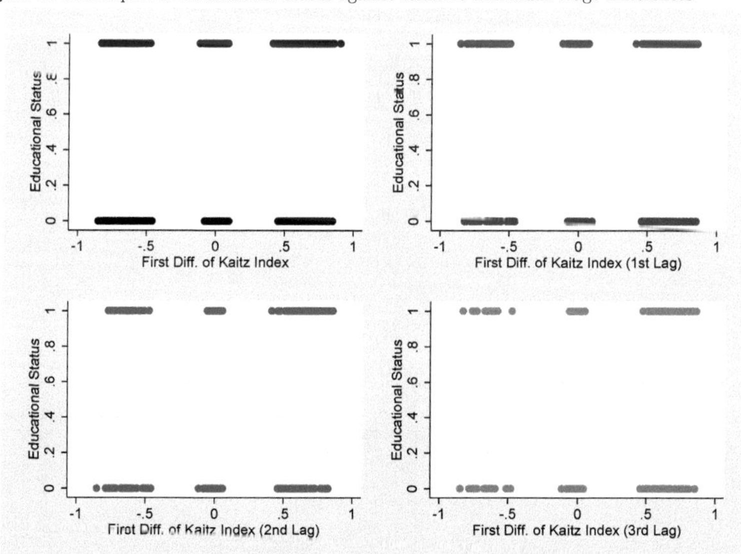

Sources: GSOEP, FSO, minimum wage regulations; author's figure

5 Regression Results

The purpose of this section is to present the evidence obtained by the regression analysis. To begin with, the fulfillment of model demands is tested. Then, baseline results are illustrated and scrutinized. This procedure is followed by several robustness checks.

5.1 Results of the Baseline Model

As a first basic attempt, a linear regression is carried out using a panel OLS approach to detect data particularities. The educational status is estimated depending on first differences of absolute minimum wages and time effects.[36] Three tests indicate a misspecification when using this standard model, see table 4.

Table 4: Results of Model Specification Testing

Test	Null Hypothesis H_0	Test Statistic	P-Value	Reject H_0?
Wald Test	Homoskedasticity	$X^2 = 2.2 \cdot 10^{35}$	0.0000	Yes
Wooldridge Test	No first order autocorrelation	$F(1, 1549) = 389.044$	0.0000	Yes
Hausman Test	Differences in coefficients are not systematic	$X^2 = 154.94$	0.0000	Yes[a]

Notes: [a] FE should be included and IIA is violated.
The modified Wald test and the Wooldridge test are based on a Panel OLS model and prove a misspecification for the present data analysis. The Hausman test is conducted for two panel logit models with random or fixed effects respectively.

Sources: GSOEP, FSO, minimum wage regulations; author's calculations

The modified Wald test for heteroskedastic residuals (cf. Greene, 2012, pp. 419-420) yields a large X^2-value, rejecting the null hypothesis of homoskedasticity at the 1%-significance level. A comparably clear result is provided by the Wooldridge test for autocorrelated residuals (cf. Wooldridge, 2010, pp. 176-177). With an F-value of 389.044, the null hypothesis of no autocorrelation is rejected at all common significance levels. With

36 For the results, see tab. C.4.

regard to the research question, it is not surprising that these requirements of a panel OLS model are not met here. As a consequence, a general least squares (GLS) model with clustered standard errors is preferable as a linear approach.[37]

The appropriate specification of a non-linear logit model for binary choices has been outlined above. Since the residuals suffer from heteroskedasticity, the CL model including FE is suitable as supposed. This specification is further supported by the Hausman test which indicates systematic differences in coefficients between a fixed and a random effects logit model, favoring the FE model (cf. tab. 4). However, the rejection of the null hypothesis also implies a violation of the IIA assumption of the CL model (cf. Greene, 2012, pp. 807-808). Therefore, the MIL approach is preferable given the present data as it is able to handle all mentioned difficulties (see section 4.1.2).

The regression estimates with respect to absolute minimum wages first are displayed in table 5.[38] The results of the linear approach show significantly positive effects of minimum wage differences both in model (1) without and in model (2) with control variables. Thus, the apprenticeship probability increases with wage floors. The coefficients are small: in case of a minimum wage difference of 1, the apprenticeship probability rises by less than one percentage point in the model without controls and by about one percentage point in the model with controls. Only the coefficient on the three-period lagged minimum wage is contrastingly negative and significant on a 5%-level. The non-linear logit approaches yield comparable results. The coefficients in the CL model are not significant and probably biased, however, at least for the first two lags of minimum wage differences in (3), the coefficients are also positive. The impact is further confirmed by the MIL model which is assumed to fit the data structure best: the estimates for the current and the one-period lagged difference are positive and significantly different from zero on a 1%-level. The coefficient on the two-period lagged difference is significant on a 5%-level.

[37] A detailed consideration of OLS assumptions is beyond the scope of this thesis. For basic information on the linear models, see Greene (2012), pp. 56, 304-306 or Wooldridge (2010), pp. 147-152, 157-159.

[38] Prior to the regression, a potential collinearity of variables has been checked, see tables C.1, C.2 and C.3. The variance inflation factors do not recommend the exclusion of regressors.

Table 5: Regression Results Using Absolute Minimum Wages

Dep. Variable: Educational Status	(1) GLS	(2) GLS	(3) CL	(4) CL	(5) MIL	(6) MIL
(Δ Minimum Wage)$_t$	0.000915***	0.00732***	0.0309	0.0182	0.0813***	0.0910***
	(0.000322)	(0.000118)	(0.0482)	(0.0575)	(0.0238)	(0.0298)
(Δ Minimum Wage)$_{t-1}$	0.00198***	0.0111***	0.00341	-0.0335	0.131***	0.125***
	(0.000479)	(0.000193)	(0.0565)	(0.0649)	(0.0344)	(0.0383)
(Δ Minimum Wage)$_{t-2}$	0.00109	0.00791***	-0.0107	-0.0292	0.0901**	0.0862**
	(0.000667)	(0.000370)	(0.0418)	(0.0467)	(0.0402)	(0.0411)
(Δ Minimum Wage)$_{t-3}$	-0.00282**	-0.00187**	-0.0348	-0.0437	-0.00262	0.00330
	(0.00120)	(0.000867)	(0.0390)	(0.0420)	(0.0503)	(0.0504)
Sex: Female		-0.0226***				-0.451**
		(0.000857)				(0.223)
Nationality: Non-German		-0.110***		0.111		-1.745***
		(0.00151)		(0.813)		(0.367)
Secondary Degree: Lower		0.163***				1.737***
		(0.00575)				(0.523)
Secondary Degree: Medium		0.235***		1.743		3.318***
		(0.00521)		(1.798)		(0.535)
(Δ State Unemployment Rate)$_{t-1}$		0.00304***		0.0547		0.00864
		(0.0000841)		(0.0882)		(0.0732)
(Δ Number of Apprenticeship Places)$_{t-1}$		-0.000345***		-0.0571***		-0.0255**
		(0.0000125)		(0.0176)		(0.0126)
(Δ Relative Youth Cohort Size)$_{t-1}$		1.060***		79.10***		13.15***
		(0.0239)		(15.09)		(2.949)
Constant	0.930***	0.572***			3.220***	0.0635
	(0.00427)	(0.00653)			(0.268)	(0.620)
Individual Intercept (Std. Dev.)					1.214***	1.121***
					(0.0379)	(0.0662)
Observations	6,571	3,753	1,352	800	8,002	1,542
Number of Groups					3,682	2,040
Controls	No	Yes	No	Yes	No	Yes
Year Effects	Yes	Yes	Yes	Yes	Yes	Yes
Sector Effects	No	No	No	No	No	No
Pseudo R-squared			0.348	0.350		

Standard errors in parentheses; *** $p<0.01$, ** $p<0.05$, * $p<0.1$

Sources: GSOEP, FSO, minimum wage regulations; author's calculations

For the three-period lagged difference, the estimate is negative in MIL model (5) without controls and positive when including controls but insignificant in both cases. Obviously, the three-period lagged variable has no clear influence on the educational status. Since an apprenticeship lasts three years, the longest minimum wage lag might be influential only for those individuals that are close to finish their training.

A closer scrutiny of GLS and MIL estimates reveals a certain time pattern. The estimates on the one- and two-period lagged differences are larger than on the current difference which supports the expectation that educational decisions as reactions to minimum wage changes are realized with a certain delay. Overall, comparing the two logit approaches, the MIL model yields higher coefficients. Unfortunately, the pseudo R-squared as a measure of fit can only be computed for the little reliable CL approach according to which the fraction of variance explained by the model is about 0.35. The standard deviation of the random individual intercept in the MIL model which exceeds 1 also points at an incomplete explanation of variance by the variables. In both MIL models, the intraclass-correlation is about 0.77. Thus, 77% of the between-variance is explained by the random intercept (cf. Rabe-Hesketh/Skrondal, 2005, p. 8).

A brief look is taken at the other explanatory variables. As already suggested by the correlation matrix, there is a significant effect of school qualifications. Both a lower and a medium secondary degree positively contribute to the probability of doing an apprenticeship whereas the estimate for the medium degree is almost twice as large. Being non-German significantly reduces the apprenticeship probability. The effect of sexes indicates a lower probability for young women and is significant on a 5%-level. All estimates on these personal characteristics are larger compared to the minimum wage coefficients. At least in the logit models, there are no significant effects of first differences of state unemployment rates. Nevertheless, the effect is positive as expected: the more unemployment grows, the higher is the willingness of youths to undergo further education and improve future employment prospects. The negative effect of the number of apprenticeship places is interpretable in a similar way. It expresses the demand for apprentices which is partly linked to the overall demand for workers: the correlation matrix displays a negative relation of changes in unemployment and changes in apprenticeship places (cf. tab. 3). Thus, the higher the demand for workers in general, the higher is the demand for apprentices, probably due to an upward economic trend. With a larger probability of finding a job, youths feel less constrained to enhance their employability by professional skill acquisition. Moreover, the argumentation is underlined by the positive educational effect of a rising relative youth cohort size. A more competitive labor market situation encourages youths to increase their employment probability by occupational training.

Table 6: Baseline Regression Results Using Relative Minimum Wages

Dep. Variable: Educational Status	(1) GLS	(2) GLS	(3) CL	(4) CL	(5) MIL	(6) MIL
(Δ Kaitz Index)$_t$	0.0437***	0.112***	0.553	0.389	1.316***	1.449***
	(0.00453)	(0.000938)	(0.627)	(0.790)	(0.340)	(0.450)
(Δ Kaitz Index)$_{t-1}$	0.0629***	0.170***	0.291	-0.230	2.094***	1.990***
	(0.00647)	(0.00159)	(0.715)	(0.848)	(0.480)	(0.563)
(Δ Kaitz Index)$_{t-2}$	0.0512***	0.108***	0.0999	-0.128	1.555***	1.508**
	(0.00918)	(0.00360)	(0.547)	(0.620)	(0.557)	(0.595)
(Δ Kaitz Index)$_{t-3}$	0.00240	-0.0429***	-0.351	-0.473	0.135	0.200
	(0.0168)	(0.0114)	(0.521)	(0.566)	(0.685)	(0.702)
Sex: Female		-0.0258***				-0.527**
		(0.000605)				(0.238)
Nationality: Non-German		-0.112***		0.113		-1.881***
		(0.000918)		(0.812)		(0.357)
Secondary Degree: Lower		0.161***				1.848***
		(0.00341)				(0.570)
Secondary Degree: Medium		0.234***		1.750		3.629***
		(0.00267)		(1.796)		(0.579)
(Δ State Unemployment Rate)$_{t-1}$		0.00290***		0.0537		0.00497
		(0.0000704)		(0.0879)		(0.0750)
(Δ Number of Apprenticeship		-0.000283***		-0.0558***		-0.0279**
Places)$_{t-1}$		(0.0000153)		(0.0176)		(0.0132)
(Δ Relative Youth Cohort Size)$_{t-1}$		1.042***		78.75***		15.24***
		(0.0250)		(15.13)		(3.140)
Constant	0.934***	0.572***			3.216***	-0.0309
	(0.00429)	(0.00490)			(0.267)	(0.670)
Individual Intercept (Std. Dev)					1.215***	1.225***
					(0.0379)	(0.0582)
Observations	6,571	3,753	1,352	800	8,062	4,512
Number of Groups					3,682	2,040
Controls	No	Yes	No	Yes	No	Yes
Year Effects	Yes	Yes	Yes	Yes	Yes	Yes
Sector Effects	No	No	No	No	No	No
Pseudo R-squared			0.348	0.350		

Standard errors in parentheses; *** p<0.01, ** p<0.05, * p<0.1

Sources: GSOEP, FSO, minimum wage regulations; author's calculations

The estimation is repeated using relative minimum wages. The results presented in table 6 differ only slightly since the correlation of absolute and relative minimum wage differences is high (cf. tab. B.7). The GLS and the MIL model produce significantly positive coefficients with and without controls. Again, the impact of the three-period lagged difference is unclear for stated reasons. Compared to the coefficients on absolute differences, the estimates increase and all exceed a value of 1 since relative differences are smaller. The time structure is unchanged, with the one- and two-period lagged differences yielding the largest coefficients. However, performing Wald tests to check for the equality of minimum wage coefficients in (6) does not yield significant results. Thus, the differences in estimates are negligibly small (cf. tab. C.5). To explain this uniformity, one can argue that the stage of an apprenticeship is neglected here so that all apprentices are treated equally regardless of how long the starting point of their training dates back.

Furthermore, the coefficients on the control variables follow the same pattern as outlined above with slightly larger estimates except for the difference of the state umemployment rate. In model (6), the coefiicient of the medium secondary degree is two times larger than the coefficient of the lower secondary degree and they are significantly different from each other (cf. tab. C.5). Referring again to the pseudo R-squared, the explanatory power seems to be unaffected. Linked to previous studies, the MIL specification using relative minimum wage differences is referred to as the baseline regression model.

Since the coefficients in a non-linear model are not intuitively interpretable, we focus on the observation of predicted values and marginal effects (ME). Table 7 summarizes the predictions made by the baseline MIL approach. The mean predicted value exceeds 0.8 in both cases which corresponds to the earlier observation that an apprenticeship is the likelier choice. The range of predictions covers the entire interval between 0 and 1.

Table 7: Summary of Predicted Values

Variable	Obs	Mean	Std. Dev.	Min	Max
Predicted Probability (without Controls)	8,062	0.8352	0.2641	0.0171	0.9985
Resulting Deviance Residual	8,062	0.0438	0.5431	-2.3485	1.8208
Predicted Probability (with Controls)	4,535	0.8518	0.2592	0.0000[a]	1.0000
Resulting Deviance Residual	4,535	0.0501	0.5931	-8.4904	7.5768

[a] Rounded Value

Sources: GSOEP, FSO, minimum wage regulations; author's calculations

A scatterplot of predictions against the educational status shows that higher predicted values tend to match higher actual values (cf. fig. 7). However, especially for the unskilled group, the wide range of predictions is clearly demonstrated. Assuming that the model correctly predicts the decision if the actual educational status is 1 (0) and the predicted value is equal or larger (smaller) than 0.5, the baseline model yields a fraction of correct predictions of 0.94 with and without controls.

Figure 7: Scatterplot of Predicted Probability against Educational Status

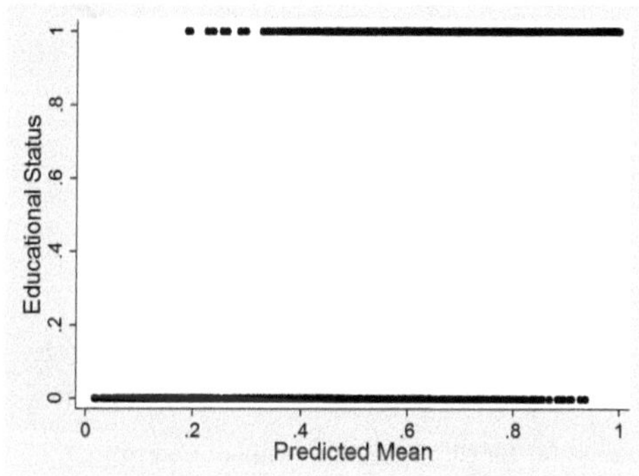

(a) Baseline Regression without Controls

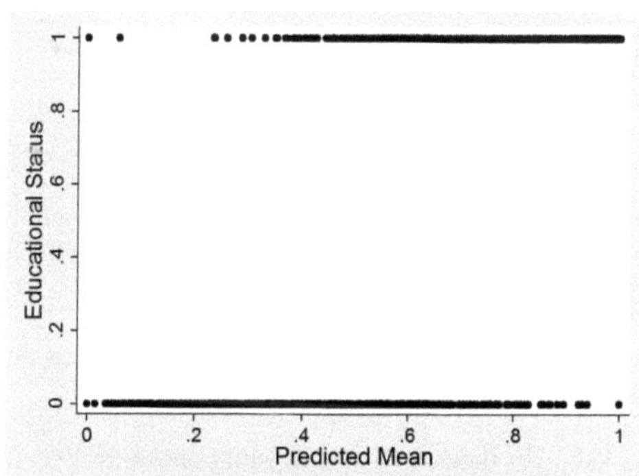

(b) Baseline Regression with Controls

Sources: GSOEP, FSO, minimum wage regulations; author's figure

Figure 8 displays a quantile-quantile-plot of deviance residuals against a standard normal distribution. In case of a well-fitted model, they are equal. Obviously, the model without controls produces a zero residual too often. By adding controls, the distributions converge to some extent; however, the range of residuals and, particularly, the number of outliers increases.

Figure 8: Quantile-Quantile-Plot of Deviance Residuals against Standard Normal Distribution

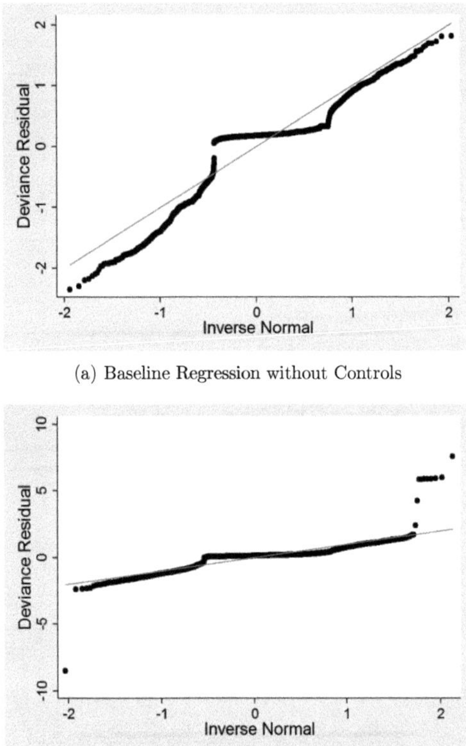

(a) Baseline Regression without Controls

(b) Baseline Regression with Controls

Sources: GSOEP, FSO, minimum wage regulations; author's figure

In total, there are 9 observations for which the absolute deviance residual exceeds 5. A closer inspection reveals that all of the concerned individuals changed their status once, switching from an unskilled employment to an apprenticeship or vice versa. Thus, both values of the dependent variable are taken up although at least the time-invariant regressors are unchanged. Therefore, the variation of the educational status cannot fully be attributed to them which leads to larger residuals.[39]

To complete the understanding of the minimum wage impact, the partial derivatives of apprenticeship probabilities with respect to the significant Kaitz index differences are considered. To compute the average impact, it is necessary to exclude the individual random intercept and rely on the non-specific portion of the MIL model only. For a one-period lagged Kaitz difference of 0.1, the mean apprenticeship probability rises by about 0.68 and 0.71 percentage points respectively (cf. tab. 8) which matches the small ME seen in the linear approach. Combining the result with the sample mean of the one-period lagged Kaitz difference which is 0.034 (cf. tab. 2), the average contribution to the apprenticeship probability is less than 0.3 percentage points.

Table 8: Marginal Effects of Minimum Wage Differences

Variable	Marginal Effect	Std. Err.	P-Value
Baseline Regression without Controls (N=8,062)			
$(\Delta \text{ Kaitz Index})_t$	0.0447	0.0125	0.000
$(\Delta \text{ Kaitz Index})_{t-1}$	0.0711	0.0181	0.000
$(\Delta \text{ Kaitz Index})_{t-2}$	0.0528	0.0198	0.008
Baseline Regression with Controls (N=4,542)			
$(\Delta \text{ Kaitz Index})_t$	0.0495	0.0166	0.003
$(\Delta \text{ Kaitz Index})_{t-1}$	0.0679	0.0213	0.001
$(\Delta \text{ Kaitz Index})_{t-2}$	0.0515	0.0214	0.016

Sources: GSOEP, FSO, minimum wage regulations; author's calculations

It is emphasized that the lagged differences of the Kaitz index should not be regarded as completely independent of each other. For example, a change of the one-period lagged difference only leaves either the two-period lagged difference or the current difference unaffected. Thus, in combination with ME of other lags, the impact may be somewhat different.

39 Since the large residuals are not caused by an error-in-variables, the respective observations are further included. Dropping them yields no substantial differences in estimates.

Figure 9: Mean Predicted Probabilities, Baseline Regression Sample

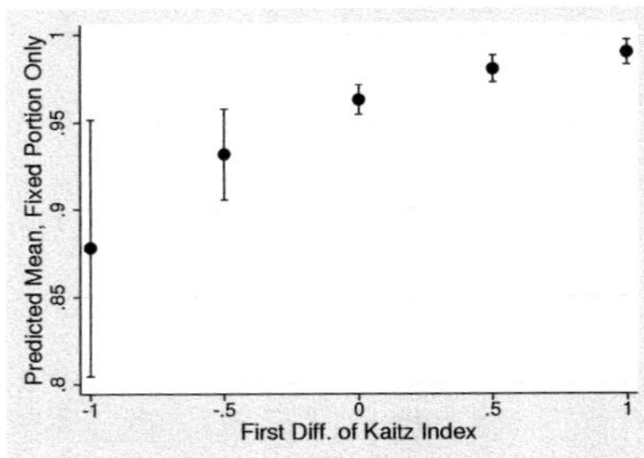

(a) Current Value, No Controls

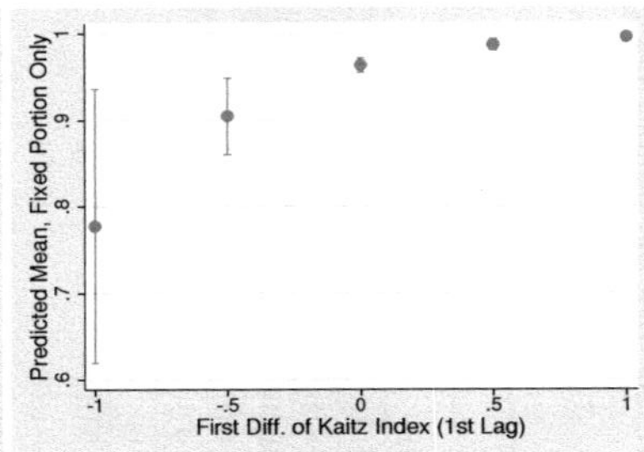

(b) 1st Lag, No Controls

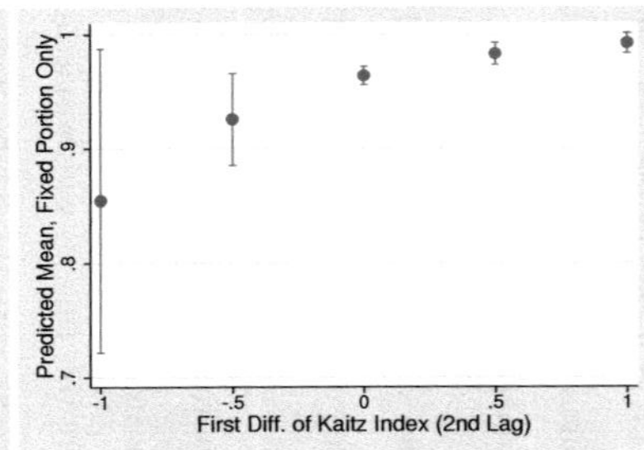

(c) 2nd Lag, No Controls

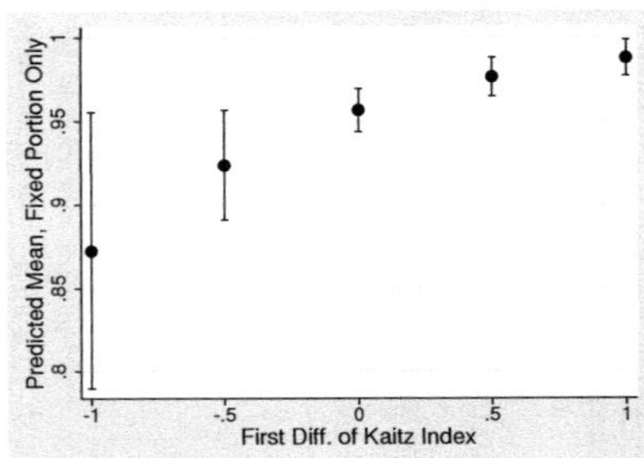

(d) Current Value, Incl. Controls

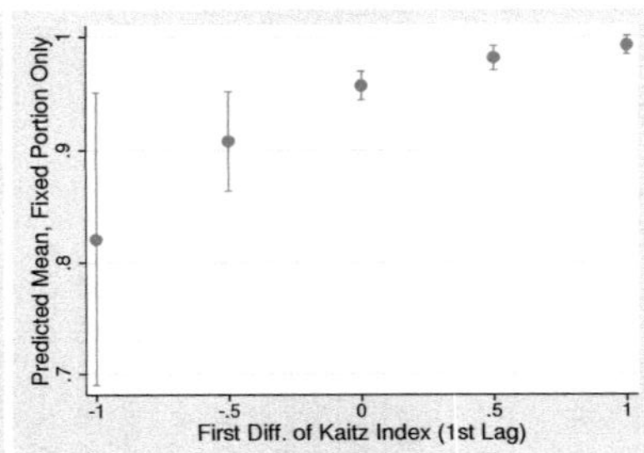

(e) 1st Lag, Incl. Controls

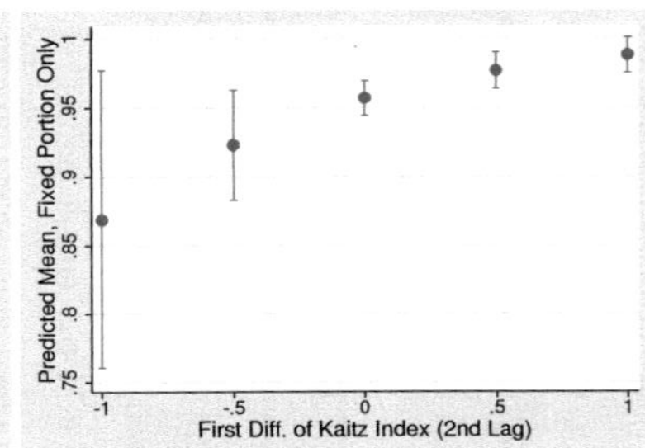

(f) 2nd Lag, Incl. Controls

Sources: GSOEP, FSO, minimum wage regulations; author's figure

In order to compare the effects of minimum wage differences, the predicted probabilities at certain cut-off values are shown in figure 9. Again, the predictions do not take account of the individual heterogeneity. The mean predicted probability is displayed with the Kaitz index difference taking up the stated value between -1 and 1 while keeping all other regressors at their sample means. With larger minimum wage differences, predictions rise according to the regression coefficients. Furthermore, the lenghts of 95%-confidence intervals diminish since predictions converge to 1. As the coefficient on the one-period lagged Kaitz index is largest, predictions have the widest range.[40]

Strikingly, even with the highest possible relative minimum decrease of -1, the predicted probability is always greater than 0.77. Conclusively, the fraction of apprentices would still be more than three times larger than the fraction of unskilled workers. Compared to the actual sample mean of 0.81, this is a reduction by only 4 percentage points. Against that, a strong increase of wage floors leads to mean predictions close to 1. Thus, a higher minimum wage affects the decision positively; however, the average preference for education largely outweighs that for unskilled employment anyway. Therefore, a hypothetical total elimination of minimum wages provokes no sharp drop.

The importance of personal characteristics has been outlined for what reason mean probabilities are also computed for sexes and school qualifications at the indicated values of Kaitz differences. The upper row of figure 10 illustrates a higher apprenticeship probability for males compared to females. Nonetheless, the sex differences account for maxima of four to six percentage points and fall with increasing changes of the relative minimum wage. Thus for a Kaitz difference of 1, mean predicted probabilities differ by less than one percentage point regardless of the lag considered. Again, the high disposition to professional education is shown for both sexes since mean predictions exceed 0.7 even for the largest reduction of relative minimum wages.

40 For all predictions of the baseline model, see tables C.6 and C.7.

Figure 10: Mean Predicted Probabilities for Subgroups

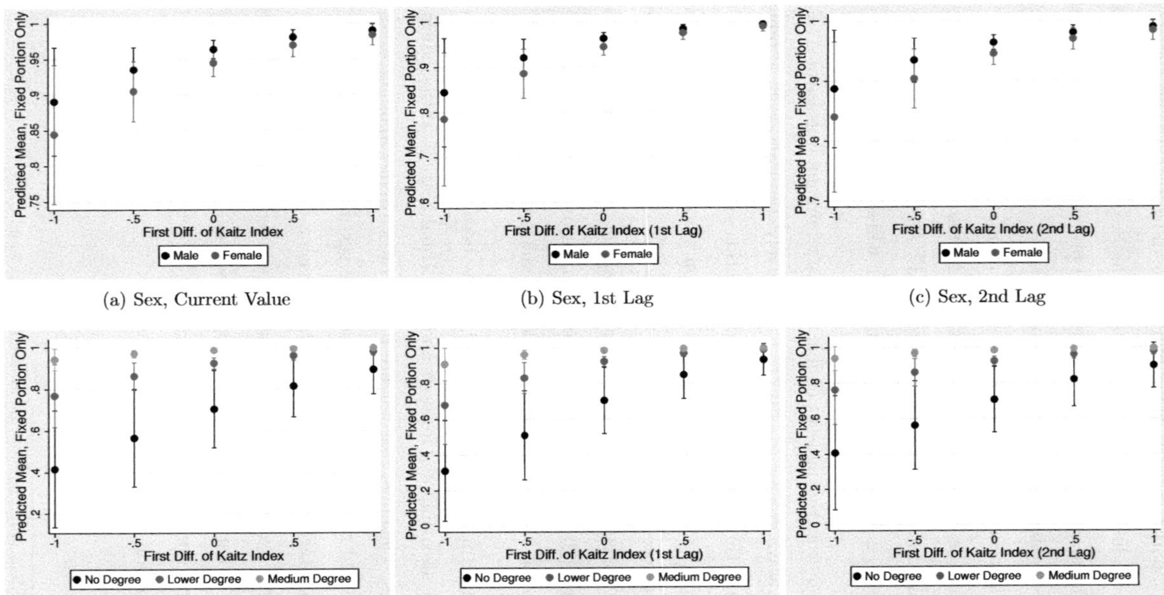

(a) Sex, Current Value (b) Sex, 1st Lag (c) Sex, 2nd Lag

(d) School Degree, Current Value (e) School Degree, 1st Lag (f) School Degree, 2nd Lag

Sources: GSOEP, FSO, minimum wage regulations; author's figure

Stronger contrasts are observable considering school degrees. For individuals with no school degree, the model predicts a mean apprenticeship probability of 0.31 with a one-period lagged Kaitz difference of -1. Facing the same influence, the predicted probability of medium secondary graduates is at 0.91.[41] On the contrary, for strong minimum increases, the gap in predictions shrinks to a maximum of 10 percentage points. Hence, the apprenticeship probability strongly depends on initial qualifications. For the group without a degree, the minimum wage can even have an altering effect on the decision. In contrast, the apprenticeship disposition of school-leavers with a medium degree is barely changed by wage floor variations. Evidently, setting additional incentives for education by means of a minimum wage closes the respective gender gap but not the gap between school degrees.

Although the imputed minimum wage differences are rather artificial and the individual intercept is excluded, the analysis clearly demonstrates the different effects for specific subgroups according to characteristics which influence the educational status. The significant disparities confirm the respective evidence obtained by previous studies (cf. Ehrenberg/Marcus, 1982; Landon, 1997; Mincer/Leighton, 1980).

These observations lead over to another model expansion. Since sectoral minimum wages are analyzed here, it appears reasonable to take sector effects into account.[42] Notably, the explanation power of the model is positively affected, see table 9. The pseudo R-squared in CL model (3) rises by 0.11, compared to the regression without sector components. The significantly positive minimum wage effect remains. Furthermore, the MIL coefficients on the Kaitz differences rise by 0.1 up to 0.3 compared to the baseline model. The GLS models (1) and (2) now show a signficantly positive effect of the three-period lagged Kaitz difference as well. The coefficients on sexes and determinants of labor markt competivity

---

41 For all values of predicted probabilities, see tables C.8, C.9 and C.10.

42 Due to the fact that the NACE sector takes up 100 different manifestations, an inclusion of both sector and time dummies is hardly possible in the logit models, especially in case of a further reduction of variance by control variables. Therefore, the permanent use of both effects is abstained from.

are insignificant in column (6), probably because the influences are partly captured by the sector effects.

Table 9: Regression Results Including Sectoral Effects

Dep. Variable: Educational Status	(1) GLS	(2) GLS	(3) CL	(4) CL	(5) MIL	(6) MIL
(Δ Kaitz Index)$_t$	0.107***	0.120***	0.934	1.525	1.365***	1.367***
	(0.00291)	(0.00248)	(0.942)	(0.995)	(0.356)	(0.451)
(Δ Kaitz Index)$_{t-1}$	0.143***	0.150***	0.509	1.482	2.333***	2.168***
	(0.00411)	(0.00324)	(0.962)	(0.902)	(0.485)	(0.565)
(Δ Kaitz Index)$_{t-2}$	0.113***	0.124***	-0.393	1.041	1.728***	1.593***
	(0.00723)	(0.00233)	(0.605)	(0.739)	(0.560)	(0.592)
(Δ Kaitz Index)$_{t-3}$	0.0554***	0.0269***	-0.466	0.395	0.463	0.357
	(0.0152)	(0.00395)	(0.503)	(0.691)	(0.695)	(0.707)
Sex: Female		-0.0164***				-0.398
		(0.00140)				(0.243)
Nationality: Non-German		-0.123***		1.668***		-1.736***
		(0.00134)		(0.520)		(0.353)
Secondary Degree: Lower		1.014***				1.881***
		(0.000474)				(0.566)
Secondary Degree: Medium		1.049***		-0.236		3.629***
		(0.00160)		(1.433)		(0.574)
(Δ State Unemployment Rate)$_{t-1}$		0		0.0339		0.0343
		(0)		(0.0831)		(0.0562)
(Δ Number of Apprenticeship Places)$_{t-1}$		-0.00183***		-0.00970***		-0.00306
		(0.0000638)		(0.00332)		(0.00245)
(Δ Relative Youth Cohort Size)$_{t-1}$		0.239***		0.438**		-0.0312
		(0.00802)		(0.223)		(0.180)
Constant	0.843***	0			117.5***	329.2***
	(0.00566)	(0)			(30.96)	(57.39)
Individual Intercept (Std. Dev.)					1.224***	1.198***
					(0.0386)	(0.0594)
Observations	6,261	3,585	1,276	773	7,516	4,364
Number of Groups					3,360	1,984
Controls	No	Yes	No	Yes	No	Yes
Year Effects	Yes	Yes	Yes	No	Yes	Yes
Sector Effects	Yes	Yes	Yes	Yes	Yes	Yes
Pseudo R-squared			0.470	0.199		

Standard errors in parentheses; *** $p<0.01$, ** $p<0.05$, * $p<0.1$

Notes: Due to computational effort, time and sectoral effects are specified as non-factor variables in the MIL models here.

Sources: GSOEP, FSO, minimum wage regulations; author's calculations

Apparently, sector-specific characteristics make an important contribution to the set of exogenous influences. In particular, they can represent the required skill level: with an occupation demanding special qualifications, youths are likelier to acquire those to improve their employment prospects. Thus, in addition to the educational incentives set by wage floors, occupational requirements have an encouraging effect. This finding gives rise to the question of whether wage floors induce different effects among sectors depending on skill standards. Beyond simply controlling for sectoral effects, a sector-specific analysis might provide results of higher precision and reliability.

Unfortunately, GSOEP data on single occupational groups is limited, in some cases to only a one- or two-digit number of observations. Thus, conducting a separate analysis is hardly feasible. Nevertheless, an attempt is performed for those minimum wage groups which provide the most observations: main construction trades, electrical trades and care nursing. Yet, the samples are still too small to conduct another but the GLS regression. Table 10 contains the results. The estimates tendencially agree with the hypothesis of different minimum wage impacts. The effects are significantly positive for main construction trades and electrical trades but significantly negative for care nursing. In order to reveal the true sector-specific effects, further investigation is required.

Table 10: Attempt of Sector-Specific Regressions

	(1)	(2)	(3)
Dep. Variable: Educational Status	GLS	GLS	GLS
	Main Constr. Trades	Care Nursing	Electr. Trades
$(\Delta \text{ Kaitz Index})_t$	0.427***	0.151***	0.0887*
	(0.0490)	(0.0549)	(0.0458)
$(\Delta \text{ Kaitz Index})_{t-1}$	0.469***	-0.136**	0.0844*
	(0.0509)	(0.701)	(0.0298)
$(\Delta \text{ Kaitz Index})_{t-2}$	0.441***	-1.898***	0.8102*
	(0.0480)	(0.2490)	(0.0432)
$(\Delta \text{ Kaitz Index})_{t-3}$	0.314**	–	0.0620
	(0.0546)	–	(0.0403)
Constant	0.903***	-49.527***	0.999***
	(0.0215)	(1.6447)	(0.0034)
Observations	489	101	458
Controls	No	No	No
Year Effects	Yes	Yes	Yes

Standard errors in parentheses; *** p<0.01, ** p<0.05, * p<0.1

Notes: Due to the small sample size, continuous time effects are included in care nursing.

Sources: GSOEP, FSO, minimum wage regulations; author's calculations

Having observed a small positive overall impact in the baseline regression, the question of its robustness is yet to answer. Therefore, the model specification is now changed in order to check if the effects remain stable.

5.2 Robustness Checks

The sensitivity analysis is divided into two parts. In a first step, selected variables are added or replaced. As a second check, the estimation sample is modified whereas both a decrease and an increase in size occur.

5.2.1 Variations of Variables

For the first check, sectoral wage floors are now captured by the indicator of minimum wage existence. This specification is similar to a difference-in-difference approach discussed earlier (cf. Antòn/Muñoz de Bustillo, 2011; Rice, 2010). Actually, this method is not expected to improve the results since the variation among individuals is reduced and the mere existence of a minimum wage implies no information about the degree of affection. Accordingly, the results are ambigous: the GLS and the MIL models yield significantly positive estimates for the current minimum wage impact and significantly negative estimates for the longer lags (cf. tab. 11).

This inconsistency is possibly caused by the association of equal values to sectors which show different reactions to wage floors. Notably, all studies working with a minimum wage indicator do no solely rely on it but estimate the effect of its interaction with a minimum wage value. Thus evidently, the simple existence of a wage floor is litte meaningful for educational decisions which supports the baseline approach (cf. Antòn/Muñoz de Bustillo, 2011; Pacheco/Cruickshank, 2007; Rice, 2010). Furthermore, the eventual overrepresentation of sectors with long-existing minimum wages might play a role here. Hence, the coefficients for longer lags of minimum wage differences basically represent the effects in certain, single sectors that first introduced wage floors (see limitations later). No clear impact is determined when capturing minimum wages by a simple indicator variable. However, the effects of the control variables are stable and close in size to the baseline approach.

Table 11: Alternative Regression 1, Minimum Wage Dummies

Dep. Variable: Educational Status	(1) GLS	(2) GLS	(3) CL	(4) CL	(5) MIL	(6) MIL
Minimum Wage Existence$_t$	-0.00402	0.0491***	0.0885	-0.0881	0.501**	0.481*
	(0.00261)	(0.000959)	(0.458)	(0.581)	(0.233)	(0.288)
Minimum Wage Existence$_{t-1}$	-0.00277	0.0181***	-0.545	-0.808*	0.135	-0.0312
	(0.00306)	(0.00116)	(0.391)	(0.469)	(0.310)	(0.358)
Minimum Wage Existence$_{t-2}$	-0.0326***	-0.0446***	-0.418	-0.255	-0.767**	-0.709*
	(0.00444)	(0.00347)	(0.408)	(0.441)	(0.363)	(0.380)
Minimum Wage Existence$_{t-3}$	-0.168***	-0.176***	-0.645	-0.566	-1.957***	-1.897***
	(0.0137)	(0.0148)	(0.583)	(0.653)	(0.435)	(0.440)
Sex: Female		-0.0392***				-0.562**
		(0.00156)				(0.225)
Nationality: Non-German		-0.113***		0.0934		-1.717***
		(0.00311)		(0.789)		(0.369)
Secondary Degree: Lower		0.182***				1.801***
		(0.0123)				(0.520)
Secondary Degree: Medium		0.253***		1.751		3.347***
		(0.0120)		(1.739)		(0.531)
(Δ State Unemployment Rate)$_{t-1}$		0.00353***		0.0518		0.00880
		(0.0000652)		(0.0863)		(0.0731)
(Δ Number of Apprenticeship Places)$_{t-1}$		-0.000479***		-0.0583***		-0.0249*
		(0.0000335)		(0.0180)		(0.0127)
(Δ Relative Youth Cohort Size)$_{t-1}$		0.914***		76.13***		11.75***
		(0.0327)		(14.86)		(2.958)
Constant	0.906***	0.589***			2.584***	0.305
	(0.00517)	(0.0132)			(0.225)	(0.619)
Individual Intercept (Std. Dev)					1.227***	1.112***
					(0.0356)	(0.0673)
Observations	7,140	3,753	1,439	800	8,662	4,542
Number of Groups					3,914	2,040
Controls	No	Yes	No	Yes	No	Yes
Year Effects	Yes	Yes	Yes	Yes	Yes	Yes
Sector Effects	No	No	No	No	No	No
Pseudo R-squared			0.369	0.353		

Standard errors in parentheses; *** p<0.01, ** p<0.05, * p<0.1

Sources: GSOEP, FSO, minimum wage regulations; author's calculations

The alternative capture of education by the modified ISCED level demands to adjust the time structure: the differences of the Kaitz indices are shifted back three years to the third to fifth lag.[43] Accordingly, the other exogenous variables are included by means of their four-period lagged differences. Because of the distinct scales of measurement and estimation models, the coefficients displayed in table 12 are not directly comparable to those in the baseline regression. Nevertheless, the minimum wage impact is also positive and significant. Here, in all models, the estimates rise with minimum wage lag length

43 The inclusion of further lags too strongly reduces the number of observations.

which generally corresponds to the time structure observed before. Hence, a wage floor increase at least three years ago positively stimulates the presently highest educational level achieved. Recall that the dependent variable here takes up values between 1 and 5 which explains the absolutely larger coefficients.

Table 12: Alternative Regression 2a, Estimation of the ISCED Level (Modified)

	(1)	(2)	(3)	(4)	(5)	(6)
Dep. Variable: ISCED (Modified)	GLS	GLS	OL	OL	FE OL	FE OL
$(\Delta$ Kaitz Index$)_{t-3}$	0.254***	0.214***	2.079***	2.781***	1.203	4.104***
	(0.0120)	(0.0245)	(0.358)	(0.652)	(0.949)	(0.776)
$(\Delta$ Kaitz Index$)_{t-4}$	0.384***	0.373***	3.322***	4.091***	3.459***	6.602***
	(0.0277)	(0.0341)	(0.495)	(0.853)	(0.561)	(1.332)
$(\Delta$ Kaitz Index$)_{t-5}$	0.482***	0.363***	4.433***	5.644***	6.565***	10.17***
	(0.0286)	(0.0373)	(0.674)	(1.109)	(0.868)	(2.140)
Sex: Female		0.135***		1.366***		
		(0.00653)		(0.403)		
Nationality: Non-German		-0.00587		0.0941		
		(0.0134)		(0.524)		
Nationality						-8.304***
						(1.656)
Secondary Degree: Lower		1.399***		18.93***		
		(0.0311)		(3.544)		
Secondary Degree: Medium		1.334***		18.14***		
		(0.0310)		(3.455)		
Lower to Medium Secondary School Degree						6.639***
						(2.450)
$(\Delta$ State Unemployment Rate$)_{t-4}$		-0.00840***		-0.0961		-0.159**
		(0.000653)		(0.0913)		(0.0685)
$(\Delta$ Number of Apprenticeship Places$)_{t-4}$		0.00352***		0.0911***		0.00445
		(0.000158)		(0.0142)		(0.00277)
$(\Delta$ Relative Youth Cohort Size$)_{t-4}$		-0.997***		-28.32***		-0.0570
		(0.0420)		(4.157)		(0.136)
Constant	2.318***	0.983***				
	(0.00831)	(0.0310)				
Observations	9,650	3,734	11,324	4,251	5,400	1,970
Controls	No	Yes	No	Yes	No	Yes
Year Effects	Yes	Yes	Yes	Yes	Yes	Yes
Sector Effects	No	No	No	No	No	No
Pseudo R-squared					0.808	0.955

Standard errors in parentheses; *** $p<0.01$, ** $p<0.05$, * $p<0.1$

Notes: The FE OL model cannot deal with factor variables for what reason the effects on nationality, school degrees and time are based on the regular indicator variables or continuous variables respectively.

Sources: GSOEP, FSO, minimum wage regulations; author's calculations

Attention must be paid to the FE OL model since the pseudo R-squared is about 0.96 with controls added. This should be scrutinized carefully as it points at a meaningless estimation due to an almost perfect correlation of the modified ISCED level and one or more regressors. Step by step, the exogenous influences are excluded to find out about the highly explanatory variables. Table C.11 presents the results of a repetition without time effects. The minimum wage coefficients are still significantly positive which confirms the observed impact. However, the explained variation falls sharply, illustrated by a pseudo R-squared of only 0.03 and 0.12 respectively. Thus, differences in minimum wages only have a very limited explanation power concerning educational decisions. The rise in adequacy due to personal characteristics again indicates that these are of greater importance for the individual level of education. In particular, year effects and thus a higher age explain a rising ISCED level. The minimum wage impact can be determined as stable yet very small.

When specifying sectoral effects, it has already been discussed whether these represent the educational requirements imposed on youths. GSOEP data allows for a check since it provides information on the educational level that is needed for the current occupation of an individual. As can be seen in table 13, the estimated coefficients on relative minimum wage differences in the MIL models are stable compared to the baseline regression: for the current and the one-period lagged difference, the coefficients are positive and different from zero. However, they suggest an even smaller impact since no coefficient exceeds 2. The longer lags have no strong impact. Strikingly, the estimates in the CL model are partly significant here and point at a negative minimum wage impact. A potentially underlying reason to take account of is the computational method. While due to the individual intercept, the MIL model is able to base the estimation on all observations available, this is not the case in the CL model: it only relies on observations with non-equal manifestations of the dependent variable over time in order to determine the effect of varying exogenous influences. Thus, youths with a non-changing educational status are excluded (cf. Allison, 2009, p. 29; Rabe-Hesketh/Skrondal, 2005, p. 132).

Table 13: Alternative Regression 3, Required Education as a Control

Dep. Variable: Educational Status	(1) GLS	(2) GLS	(3) CL	(4) CL	(5) MIL	(6) MIL
$(\Delta \text{ Kaitz Index})_t$	0.0979***	0.0681***	-0.844	-1.295	1.081***	1.077***
	(0.000202)	(0.00244)	(0.769)	(0.996)	(0.388)	(0.387)
$(\Delta \text{ Kaitz Index})_{t-1}$	0.155***	0.107***	-0.821	-1.789**	1.916***	1.942***
	(0.000776)	(0.00373)	(0.779)	(0.863)	(0.530)	(0.540)
$(\Delta \text{ Kaitz Index})_{t-2}$	0.0682***	0.0516***	-1.210*	-1.802**	0.835	0.984*
	(0.00155)	(0.00169)	(0.694)	(0.741)	(0.601)	(0.590)
$(\Delta \text{ Kaitz Index})_{t-3}$	-0.0490***	-0.0778***	-1.496***	-1.999***	-0.775	-0.655
	(0.00793)	(0.00366)	(0.564)	(0.595)	(0.803)	(0.775)
Sex: Female		-0.00805***				-0.238
		(0.000600)				(0.178)
Nationality: Non-German		-0.0600***		0.887		-1.054***
		(0.00329)		(0.947)		(0.253)
Secondary Degree: Lower		0.0155***				1.602***
		(0.00177)				(0.438)
Secondary Degree: Medium		0.0743***		0.388		2.861***
		(0.00131)		(1.195)		(0.443)
$(\Delta \text{ State Unemployment Rate})_{t-1}$		0.00330***		0.165*		
		(0.000195)		(0.0926)		
$(\Delta$ Number of Apprenticeship Places$)_{t-1}$		0.00000490		-0.0507**		-0.00463**
		(0.0000262)		(0.0233)		(0.00223)
$(\Delta \text{ Relative Youth Cohort Size})_{t-1}$		0.634***		109.9***		0.496***
		(0.0317)		(12.83)		(0.149)
Required Education: Orientation	-0.329***	-0.521***	-2.131***	-3.482***	-3.505***	-4.265***
	(0.00587)	(0.0110)	(0.827)	(1.023)	(0.513)	(0.698)
Required Education: Introduction	-0.0328***	-0.111***	0.832	-0.690	-0.664	-1.719**
	(0.00599)	(0.0111)	(0.883)	(0.845)	(0.516)	(0.692)
Required Education: Course Training	0.0840***	-0.0270***	1.083	-0.418	1.003*	-0.451
	(0.00345)	(0.00882)	(0.975)	(1.009)	(0.543)	(0.711)
Required Education: Professional Degree	0.162***	0.0377***	2.166***	1.262	2.105***	0.847
	(0.00371)	(0.00775)	(0.734)	(0.792)	(0.476)	(0.659)
Required Education: Academic Education	0.119***	-0.0252***	-0.567	0.970	1.458	0.0654
	(0.00913)	(0.00930)	(1.408)	(0.887)	(0.929)	(1.044)
Constant	0.123***	0.777***			-2.959***	1.389*
	(0.00310)	(0.0101)			(0.578)	(0.749)
Individual Intercept (Std. Dev.)					1.100***	0.993***
					(0.0546)	(0.0621)
Observations	5,270	3,622	1,063	771	6,683	5,793
Number of Groups					3,213	2,796
Controls	No	Yes	No	Yes	No	Yes
Year Effects	Yes	Yes	Yes	Yes	No	No
Sector Effects	No	No	No	No	No	No
Pseudo R-squared			0.544	0.592		

Standard errors in parentheses; *** $p<0.01$, ** $p<0.05$, * $p<0.1$

Notes: Due to computational effort, time effects were dropped in the MIL models and no interaction effects could be observed.

Sources: GSOEP, FSO, minimum wage regulations; author's calculations

Conclusively, when only considering individuals who once switched their status, a discouraging minimum wage impact might occur, especially with little skill requirements. However, the reliability of the CL estimates is still unclear.

For the required level of education, the estimated effects meet the expectations. If no specific professional education is necessary, the apprenticeship probability is largely reduced and positive minimum wage impacts are mostly outweighed. In contrast, higher requirements involving course training or even a professional degree slightly stimulate the educational preferences in model (5). The impact of required academic education is insignificant which seems plausible in view of the fact that youths qualified for university are excluded. Despite the discussed reliability problems, the pseudo R-squared in model (3) indicates that the explanatory power almost doubles by this expansion. Thus, the educational requirements are observed to be a mainly influential variable. The minimum wage impact is still stable but declining. This confirms the impression of a secondary importance.

Finally, the earlier discussed use of household income as a proxy of family wealth does not make a contribution to the investigations. The regression results including this control variable are given in table C.15. The coefficients are mostly negative and insignificant. According to the potential misspecification, one can suppose that the variable does not serve its intended purpose. The negative impact rather points at an endogeneity problem since unskilled employment leads to higher income. However, the minimum wage coefficients little change which again supports the small positive effect on the educational decision. Thus, a meaningful variable to capture family backgrounds is yet to find.

5.2.2 Variations of Sample

Further checking the robustness, several sample variations are tested. Since the object of study is the educational decision of school-leavers without higher secondary degrees, individuals qualified for the academic track have been excluded so far. Nevertheless, youths who obtained the (Fach-)Abitur can still choose an apprenticeship or unskilled employment (cf. section 4.1.1). Re-estimating the models for all degrees, the minimum wage impact changes little, see table 14.

Table 14: Alternative Regression 4, All School Degrees

Dep. Variable: Educational Status	(1) GLS	(2) GLS	(3) CL	(4) CL	(5) MIL	(6) MIL
$(\Delta$ Kaitz Index$)_t$	0.0241***	0.107***	0.199	0.187	1.077***	1.301***
	(0.00370)	(0.00140)	(0.501)	(0.681)	(0.297)	(0.398)
$(\Delta$ Kaitz Index$)_{t-1}$	0.0512***	0.163***	0.318	-0.0947	2.028***	2.133***
	(0.00542)	(0.00195)	(0.611)	(0.723)	(0.423)	(0.509)
$(\Delta$ Kaitz Index$)_{t-2}$	0.0542***	0.116***	0.454	0.0981	1.927***	1.664***
	(0.00747)	(0.00233)	(0.539)	(0.566)	(0.504)	(0.544)
$(\Delta$ Kaitz Index$)_{t-3}$	0.00769	-0.0607***	-0.0347	-0.0743	0.516	0.353
	(0.0124)	(0.00227)	(0.538)	(0.526)	(0.602)	(0.644)
Sex: Female		-0.00182**				-0.185
		(0.000747)				(0.183)
Nationality: Non-German		-0.110***		-0.354		-1.453***
		(0.00118)		(0.854)		(0.290)
Secondary Degree: Lower		0.162***		9.471***		1.538***
		(0.00321)		(2.790)		(0.502)
Secondary Degree: Medium		0.232***		0.830		3.029***
		(0.00293)		(1.674)		(0.503)
Secondary Degree: Fachabitur		0.218***		-0.982		2.533***
		(0.00951)		(2.559)		(0.589)
Secondary Degree: Abitur		0.270***		-0.531		2.204***
		(0.00293)		(2.016)		(0.525)
$(\Delta$ State Unemployment Rate$)_{t-1}$		0.00294***		0.0651		0.0379
		(0.000136)		(0.0691)		(0.0451)
$(\Delta$ Number of Apprenticeship Places$)_{t-1}$		-0.000309***		-0.0394***		-0.00519***
		(0.0000268)		(0.0124)		(0.00196)
$(\Delta$ Relative Youth Cohort Size$)_{t-1}$		0.740***		55.57***		0.282*
		(0.0159)		(8.250)		(0.149)
Constant	0.927***	0.607***			3.268***	1.219**
	(0.00348)	(0.00398)			(0.239)	(0.488)
Individual Intercept (Std. Dev.)					1.172***	1.078***
					(0.0326)	(0.0512)
Observations	9,175	4,726	1,879	969	11,336	5,783
Number of Groups					5,267	2,667
Controls	No	Yes	No	Yes	No	Yes
Year Effects	Yes	Yes	Yes	Yes	Yes	No
Sector Effects	No	No	No	No	No	No
Pseudo R-squared			0.265	0.240		

Standard errors in parentheses; *** p<0.01, ** p<0.05, * p<0.1

Notes: Due to computational effort, time effects had to be dropped in the MIL model with controls.

Sources: GSOEP, FSO, minimum wage regulations; author's calculations

The coefficients in the GLS and MIL models are again significantly positive, showing the same pattern concerning the direction of effects and their significance. Compared to their baseline counterparts, the impacts of the one- and two-period lagged minimum wage differences increase by 0.1 up to 0.2 in MIL model (6): a potential explanation is that youths with higher secondary degrees exhibit an even greater employability as apprentices (cf. Agell/Lommerud, 1997; Neumark/Wascher, 1995a). The coefficients on school degrees are also positive as anticipated. Strikingly, the estimate for the Realschule degree is larger than for the higher secondary degrees, at least in the MIL model. Possibly, since school leavers with (Fach-)Abitur usually undergo academic training, Realschule graduates are the most common apprentices thereby yielding the largest probability. Notably, the differences in sexes is not significant for this higher-skilled sample. Referring to large educational preferences which apply to school-leavers with higher degrees, it is probably equal among females and males (cf. fig. 10a,b,c).

The analysis has already revealed a great importance of school qualifications obtained prior to professional training. Therefore, the estimation is carried out separately for the three original groups of school-leavers: individuals without a formal degree, Hauptschule graduates and Realschule graduates. In order to enable an easier comparison, table 15 only displays the MIL estimates.[44]

Considering the two groups of persons with formal school degrees, the minimum wage impact is significantly positive. Compared to the baseline regression, the estimates are again close in size since the majority of observations in the baseline sample belongs to the group of lower to medium secondary degrees. Comparing columns (4) and (6), we can see that the minimum impact is smaller for Realschule graduates. Possible explanations have already been given by the analysis of MEs: since the apprenticeship preference of Realschule graduates is very large, a wage floor raise does not substantially increase the educational motivation or employability (cf. fig. 10d,e,f).

For the sample of non-graduates, no significant effect is observable. The coefficients point at a potentially negative effect which is in line with earlier results stating that youths without a formal degree do not benefit from the substitution of workers regarding their probability of further training (cf. Mincer/Leighton, 1980). However, due to the small

44 For the other results, see tab. C.12.

Table 15: Alternative Regression 5a, Separation by School Degrees (Non-linear Approach)

	No Secondary School Degree		Hauptschule Degree		Realschule Degree	
	(1)	(2)	(3)	(4)	(5)	(6)
Dep. Variable: Educational Status	MIL	MIL	MIL	MIL	MIL	MIL
$(\Delta$ Kaitz Index$)_t$	2.198	7.943	1.476***	1.019	1.218**	1.528**
	(2.456)	(5.614)	(0.509)	(0.654)	(0.484)	(0.667)
$(\Delta$ Kaitz Index$)_{t-1}$	-0.481	11.47	2.440***	2.085**	2.122***	1.545**
	(4.406)	(9.647)	(0.785)	(0.889)	(0.644)	(0.756)
$(\Delta$ Kaitz Index$)_{t-2}$	-3.052	6.056	2.562***	1.936**	0.970	0.998
	(5.428)	(7.940)	(0.947)	(0.968)	(0.711)	(0.795)
$(\Delta$ Kaitz Index$)_{t-3}$	–	–	1.375	1.033	-0.717	-0.703
	–	–	(1.030)	(1.059)	(0.897)	(0.952)
Sex: Female		0.266		-1.209***		-0.225
		(2.157)		(0.394)		(0.328)
Nationality: Non-German		-0.741		-2.458***		-1.003
		(3.152)		(0.482)		(0.610)
$(\Delta$ State Unemployment Rate$)_{t-1}$		1.585		0.0747		-0.0587
		(2.602)		(0.117)		(0.113)
$(\Delta$ Number of Apprenticeship Places$)_{t-1}$		-0.0510		-0.0304		-0.0272
		(0.104)		(0.0233)		(0.0177)
$(\Delta$ Relative Youth Cohort Size$)_{t-1}$		14.38		21.09***		12.81***
		(20.32)		(5.235)		(4.305)
Constant	3.408***	1.149	2.778***	1.117*	4.117***	3.988***
	(1.259)	(3.558)	(0.398)	(0.662)	(0.210)	(0.615)
Individual Intercept (Std. Dev.)	1.709***	1.807***	1.210***	1.179***	1.181***	1.282***
	(0.250)	(0.479)	(0.0694)	(0.103)	(0.0514)	(0.0757)
Observations	401	114	2,759	1,490	4,902	2,938
Number of Groups	212	73	1,312	689	2,216	1,305
Controls	No	Yes	No	Yes	No	Yes
Year Effects	Yes	Yes	Yes	Yes	No	Yes
Sector Effects	No	No	No	No	No	No

Standard errors in parentheses; *** $p<0.01$, ** $p<0.05$, * $p<0.1$

Sources: GSOEP, FSO, minimum wage regulations; author's calculations

number of observations here, the estimation might be imprecise. For the great majority of observations, the minimum wage effect is stable. A similar result is observable when spilitting the sample according to the level of required education discussed earlier, see table C.13. Considering occupations with a necessary skill level of introductory training at least, the minimum wage effect is significantly positive. If no education is needed or a simple orientation suffices, the coefficients are mostly insignificant. The impression of possibly differing minimum wage effects is reinforced.

Two more sample variations are analyzed. Hitherto, the coefficients have not been allowed to vary by age. The sample under observation is based on a specific age group so that uniform effects are assumed. Most previous studies do not control for age either but check for potentially varying impacts by means of separate regressions for age cohorts (cf. Ehrenberg/Marcus, 1982; Landon, 1997; Pacheco/Cruickshank, 2007). Following them, the baseline sample is divided into three groups: the 17- to 20-year-olds, the 21- to 22-year-olds and the 23- to 24-year-olds. Since the representation of individual-specific effects is hardly feasible with few time points, only the linear approach is estimated. The results displayed in table C.14 provide evidence of no age-variant effect. For all cohorts, the estimates on the more recent Kaitz differences are significantly positive which supports the assumption of a uniform effect. Against the backdrop of the criticism of minimum exemptions, it is notable that no separate regression could be conducted for the 17- and 18-year-olds. The number of observations is limited and the mean value of the educational status is larger than 0.96 in both cases. Thus, the statement of a negligibly small group of under-aged regular workers is accurate.

Finally, it has been mentioned that a potential threat to the estimation precision is the instationarity of median wages in four federal states even after computing first differences. The regression results when excluding these states compared to the baseline results are shown in table C.16. It is obvious that the estimates do not differ substantially which implies that the inclusion of the affected states yields no bias.

All in all, the positive minimum wage effect is shown to be quite stable to variations. Notwithstanding, some issues concerning the model specifications have been presented. Therefore, the next and final step is to discuss the observed impacts in more detail and provide possible explanations referring to previous considerations. Furthermore, limitations of the analysis are presented and further investigation is motivated.

6 Discussion of the Empirical Evidence

6.1 Interpretation of the Results

The state of argumentation prior to the empirical analysis can be summed up as follows: although the youth exemptions from the new German statutory minimum wage seem to be reasonable according to the international evidence, the literature also suggests a potentially non-negative impact in Germany because of specific activating labor market features. The regression results and sensitivity checks confirm the supposition: a small positive educational effect of minimum wages has been revealed. The impact is significant and mainly stable, indicating that the more absolute or relative minimum wages rise, the higher is the apprenticeship probability of youths aged 17 to 24. School-leavers are encouraged to undergo professional education instead of entering the labor market as unskilled workers. Higher coefficients on lagged than on current minimum wage differences are reported since the respective choices are not instantly realized. Thus, the observations of the German labor market reject the international evidence. The question of underlying reasons and consequences for the design of the minimum wage regulation immediately arises.

Combining the findings from all estimations, the positive educational effect of minimum wages is not classified as an unconditionally enhanced appreciation of labor suppliers for further education but as a reaction to the requirements imposed by the demand side. This supposition is motivated by two arguments. First, with respect to the theoretical foundations, the positive educational effect of minimum wages serves as evidence of the Substitution Hypothesis. If low-skilled employees who are applicable to wage floors are replaced by workers with higher qualifications, youths perceive a declining employment probability in case of remaining unskilled. Thus, following the optimization process described in section 2.1, the benefits of further education outweigh the minimum wage gains. Youths feel the need to accumulate further skills and improve their future employment prospects. A higher preference for education can therefore be determined as a reaction to the new labor demand situation. This reasoning is the same for all youth workers which causes the wage floor impact to be stable for distinct age groups. Hence, the substitution of low-skilled workers due to a minimum wage actually encourages youths in Germany to undergo further education and is not outweighed by an opposing queuing behavior as it is observed in other countries (cf. section 2.2).

Great support for this interpretation is provided by the orientation towards the required level of education. The analysis yields significant evidence of an increasing apprenticeship probability in case of higher necessary skills to carry out an occupation (cf. tab. 13). As far as the CL estimation is reliable, the explanation of variance by the model substantially improves which illustrates the importance of this exogenous influence. Conclusively, when making an occupational decision, youths are guided more by the quality of work that employers ask for than by the quantity. In order to explain the behavior, we relate to the German labor market characteristics: the apprenticeship model is a common and widespread form of professional education (cf. Acemoglu/Pischke, 1998; Riphahn, 2002). Thus, youths are offered a readily accessible and accepted possibility to learn a profession. There is no mutally exclusive distinction of education and employment that forces youths to choose only one alternative. Consequently, the system supports German labor market agents in establishing skilled employment relations. One additional point has been made by Agell/Lommerud (1997): they argue that in case of a high generality of skills, labor suppliers are further encouraged to acquire those since their knowledge is not bound to one firm (cf. Agell/Lommerud, 1997). Due to the public regulations, professional education received by apprenticeship training is mainly general within the scope of an occupation which stimulates the educational disposition. Thus, school-leavers knowing about these future benefits are willing to accept the training offers.

What results from a closer scrutiny of the effects further confirms the stability of the apprenticeship preference: despite being statistically significant, the minimum wage impact is small. A relative wage floor rise of 10 percentage points increases the average apprenticeship probability by less than one percentage point in the baseline model. Although the empirical approaches are not exactly comparable, the effect is smaller in absolute value than those found by Ehrenberg/Marcus (1982) or Neumark/Wascher (1995a, 1995b, 2003). As it has been mentioned earlier, a higher gainable wage is only a secondary influence for school-leavers in Germany: it is rather confirming an occupational decision already made than altering it. In line with this is the observation of similar mean probabilities in minimum wage groups and other occupations (cf. fig. 2c). Thus, the willingness to undergo further education when entering the labor market is generally applying to the majority of youths. Therefore, it barely reacts to short-time variations of exogenous circumstances, such as minimum wages. Furthermore, the analysis provided evidence of the fact that youths do consider the competitive situation on the labor market with regard to their own employment prospects. The overall unemployment rate of other workers has no significant impact. Again, the probability of finding a job can be determined as primarily influential. In conclusion, the decision to pursue an unskilled career must be due to other influences.

Some potential determinants have been highlighted: the analysis clarified the significance of the initially obtained skill level prior to working life. In particular, youths without a formal school degree fall behind those with higher school qualifications (cf. tab. 15, fig. 10). On the one hand, by a higher degree, the latter reveal their appreciation of education which is expressed later on by beginning a professional training. On the other hand, following the argumentation above, an employers' preference for youth workers with higher school degrees reinforces the assumption of substitution behavior. Even without a minimum wage, employers favor better qualified applicants, probably because they consider them more talented and more productive. This argument is statistically illustrated by the large positive effects of higher school degrees. Better qualified school-leavers are more attractive future employees who are considered worthwhile to invest in by offering them professional training. Thus, labor suppliers who are willing to meet the educational requirements and who are likely to succeed in achieving them are favored (cf. Agell/Lommerud, 1997). Given the evidence, we can speak of a reinforcement of this selection process by minimum wages (cf. tab. 14, 15).

At last, a lower apprenticeship probability for females and non-German youths has been observed. As these features, contrasting with school degrees, are basically not influential on productivity, the supposition of discrimination against those groups emerges. However, the analysis of respective issues is not a subject of the present thesis. All in all, the analysis illustrates that a negative minimum wage effect on employment probabilities outweighs higher gainable rewards. Thereby, it sets positive educational incentives for youths. Though, the investigations could not provide evidence on whether the positive impact applies to every sector. The attempt of a sectoral analysis suggests that the apprenticeship probability might decline in certain occupational groups, probably in those with low skill standards. Here, the strong guidance by required education induces a decline of the apprenticeship probability which is larger than a positive minimum stimulus (cf. tab. 13). More specific data on single occupations is necessary to examine the potential existence of queuing behavior and educational disincentives in low-skilled jobs. Hereby, it will also be clarified whether the observed effect here is in fact close to zero or the sum of contrary impacts.

As an alternative explanation which rather refers to horizontal educational decisions, the positive minimum wage impact can be interpreted as a result of an increased attractivity of affected occupations. While without wage floors, some occupations match individuals' talents or interests, low payment prospects discourage youths to tie themselves to this sector. However with a higher wage, the occupation is regarded as worthwhile to be carried out from a financial point of view as well. To further analyze this hypothesis, sector-specific apprenticeship opportunities could be considered. An enhanced preference for minimum wage occupations manifests in a larger number of applicants or a reduction in unoccupied apprenticeship places. Again, the need for investigation on occupation level is emphasized. Finally, the absence of a negative educational effect can emerge from the adequate setting of sectoral minimum wages. Since wage floors are the solution of a bargaining involving labor demand and supply side in the respective occupational group, they are likely to take up a value that is still acceptable for employers without a strong pressure for restructuring their labor force. The high correlations of absolute and relative minimum wages indicate that the wage floors in fact reflect regional economic variations and thereby produce moderate degrees of affection. Thus, negative consequences for employment and fundamental changes of educational incentives are prevented. At this point, reference can be made to the mostly insignificant employment effect of sectoral minimum wages (cf. Boockmann et al., 2013; Frings, 2013; Möller, 2012) which might be reasoned by the same argumentation.

However, even under the inclusion of fixed time and sectoral effects, the total variation among educational decision-makers could not be explained by the variables included. This indicates the omission of further influences, especially of unobservable ones. In connection with the arguments just outlined, social norms might be a conceivable impact. In addition to the imposition of educational requirements from the employers' side, youths may feel obliged to undergo professional education after having finished school since this is actually established as a social norm (cf. Franz/Soskice, 1995). The involatility of apprenticeship dispositions, the guidance by skill requirements and the relatively small correlation of demand for apprentices and labor demand in general, indicate that vocational training is the common school-to-work-transition and little affected by labor market reforms or business cycle issues. Accordingly, with respect to the fact that the apprenticeship probability varies with gender and nationality, further unobserved determinants are role models or social expectations on single groups that mark obstacles to education. All these findings yield the deduction of an educational decision being a complex process which is subject to many influences. At that, financial benefits are secondary to social incentives and individual aptitude or interest. Thus, the introduction of a minimum wage is not stated a crucial determinant of youths' decisions.

Referring to the research question of whether an educational effect of minimum wages exists in Germany, the answer is affirmative. Compared to the majority of the previous literature, the effect runs in the opposite direction and is positive. However, the described exceptions of youths from the general minimum have been made assuming that educational incentives are decreasing. This concern cannot be supported by the evidence here. Notwithstanding, the youth exceptions should not automatically be classified as unnecessary for the following reasons.

Taking a look at the exception of apprentices first, the argumentation above is based on the existence of substitution. If employers replace parts of their low-skilled work force by initially comparably qualified apprentices, they do so because the latter group is less costly (cf. Franz/Soskice, 1995). Consequently if applicable for wage floors, apprentices lose their advantage over low-skilled adult workers. Thus, employers face no incentive to favor them anymore. Taking potential dismissal costs into account (cf. Cahuc/Zylberberg, 2004, pp. 739-741), employers are not only indifferent but prefer keeping their incumbent workers. The extension of apprenticeship opportunities is prevented, some places might even be cut. As this scenario is incompatible with the policy aim to stimulate educational activities, it is avoided by youth exemptions. Furthermore, the outcome illustrates why minimum wages should not be misunderstood as an instrument to increase the level of education. Assuming that the higher willingness to do an apprenticeship is correctly determined a reaction to labor demand shifts, incentives are not directly set. Because of this interdependence, the demand side must not be disregarded and youth minimum wages lead to reduced opportunities for professional education. The evidence obtained is an indicator of substitution but no proof. However, a simple preference shift concerning the quality of newly employed workers can be subsumed under the term of substitution as well. Employers do not necessarily replace incumbent workers but redefine skill standards for new hires. Even in case of a missing substitution behavior, the minimum wage effect on the demand for apprentices would still be negative following basic economic rules of a falling demand at increasing prices. Therefore, in order to ensure that apprenticeship opportunities are not reduced, an exogenous wage raise should be avoided. The exemption can be judged as reasonable.

On the contrary, the same cannot be stated when considering the exception of the under-aged. As the analysis illustrated, the respective number of workers is small (cf. section 5.2.2, tab. C.14). Looking at the labor market activities of different age groups, the main activity of under-agers is being inactive, probably going to school. Looking at the individual labor status in the GSOEP, less than 1% of available observations is classified as under-aged full-time workers (cf. tab. B.3). Following the legislative's reasoning, the minimum wage exception serves at keeping this group small and at preventing the under-aged apprentices from giving up their training. However, considering the educational status variable again, the mean age of apprentices exceeds 19 years in 1990 and even rises by more than one year until 2013 (cf. fig. D.3). Thus, with a usual apprenticeship duration of three years, the mean starting age is likely to be higher than 18. Recalling that the fraction of youths obtaining higher secondary degrees rises (cf. fig. 3), schooling prolongs. To completely rule out negative educational incentives, the exception would have to be extended to cover older youths as well. As the upper limit, the mean age at completion of vocational training could be imposed. For example, youths obtaining a higher secondary degree finish school at the age of 18 or 19. So they usually would have finished a three-year apprenticeship training at the age of 21 or 22. By setting a respective age limit, the full-aged fraction of youth apprentices is also prevented from potentially negative educational effects. In fact, the analysis has shown neither a negative nor an age-variant educational impact. However to take precautions, one can argue that a minimum wage exception covering the entire youth cohort is adequate. In every case, the exception should only refer to those not having completed professional training, otherwise further negative incentives to begin or finish professional education are set in turn.

Despite the fact that the research question can be answered by means of the empirical evidence, the concerns over the adequate level of analysis have not been overcome yet. As discussed, the regression results point at an influence of sectoral characteristics. In case of both positive and negative educational effects of minimum wages, the critics of a youth minimum wage could rely on an argument similar to that urged above: the sectoral ambiguity of wage floor effects is in favor of a general inapplicability of youths up to an adequate age limit. Negative effects would be prevented and so is an undesirable discrimination against some youths by exempting only certain negatively affected occupations. In contrast, direct educational support can be used to promote skill acquisition. Feasible measures are higher financial transfers for apprentices, cost takeovers for material or state funding given to professional schools. This way, educational incentives are positively stimulated while wages are left untouched.

Consequently, regardless of possibly varying educational effects, an arguable strategy in each case is to exempt youths from wage floors to a wide extent and thereby leave their educational incentives and opportunities unchanged, at least with respect to vertical shifts. Although the main object of study have been sectoral minimum wages, the outcomes can be transferred to the general one. Depending on the degree of affection, the decisions of youths are subject to positive or negative incentives to train in a certain occupation. Thus, to provide evidence on educational impacts including the uniform statutory wage floor, a sector-specific analysis appears to be a reasonable approach as well.

All in all, the obtained results confirm the argumentation of Neumark/Wascher (2004) stating that labor market features and institutions yield different minimum wage effects. Compared to the mostly negative impact from other countries, the analysis here provides evidence of an opposing effect. As Neumark/Wascher supposed, the positive impact of minimum wages can be attributed to an activating labor market in Germany, offering an estabilished system of professional education which is reinforced by the outlined social norms interacting with policy measures. Although having estimated mainly stable effects here, the analysis stimulates some new issues. Further investigation on sector level is needed not only to determine the actual directions of educational effects but to also reveal the complementarity or contrariness of labor market policies when it comes to distinct technical and economic contexts. Thus, minimum wage exceptions for youth employees can be supported even though the general evidence contrasts with the literature that suggests the inapplicability. In any case, a minimum wage exception bears the advantage of avoiding new incentive structures and reoptimizations on both sides of labor market participants. To summarize, it can be stated that the overall educational effect of minimum wages in Germany is positive and small. Since this is attributed to the apprenticeship system, the youth exceptions are classified as useful measures against a reduction of apprenticeship opportunities. However, a need for improvement regarding their coverage has been exposed. For full understanding, the impact on lower economy levels should be subject to closer scrutiny.

6.2 Limitations

Despite the stable evidence obtained, some difficulties considering the data or estimation methods cannot be avoided. This section sheds light on shortcomings that are to remember when interpreting the results.

The estimation sample is constituted by the association of minimum wages and individuals which is described in section 4.2.2. The information on occupations in the GSOEP is precise and easily comparable with occupational labels given in minimum wage regulations. However, as no direct individual statement on the applicability is provided, the case that individuals are matched with a wage floor that is in fact invalid for them cannot be ruled out completely. Furthermore, the representation of sector effects is a problem as well: as mentioned earlier, sectoral characteristics are included by controlling for the NACE sector an individual works in. On the one hand, the variable is useful since it provides a uniform and all-inclusive classification of economic fields. However, as the NACE sectors and the minimum wage groups are not completely coherent, the former consist of both individuals who are applicable to a statutory minimum wage and those who are not. Thus, the NACE sectors capture occupation-specific effects which are not exclusively applying to minimum wage workers. However, using this method appears preferable over treating the occupational groups without wage floors as one homogenous sector.

A second shortcoming refers to the fact that, despite the extensive dataset, some estimations are based on a limited number of observations. Therefore, carrying out potentially useful analyses for subsamples such as single occupational groups is hardly feasible. Furthermore, as could be seen when trying to run sector-specific regressions, the numbers of observations for single sectors are unequal. Thus, there may be of an overrepresentation of certain groups. The GSOEP actually provides a weighing scheme that can be applied to project empirical results to the entire population and generate realistic ratios of group sizes (cf. Frick/Haisken-DeNew, 2005, pp. 37-40). However for the purpose of this analysis, information from other sources has been added so that the data under scrutiny is not purely GSOEP-based. It is unclear whether the weighing scheme has to be adjusted to such data base modifications. Therefore, the weighing process has been left out. Thus, the actual weight of certain observations and the respective minimum wage effects can be different in reality.

Another related issue are the varying periods of use of sectoral minimum wages. While wage floors have been applied for 18 years in main construction trades, they have only been used for five years in waste management. Thus, it must be regarded that groups that first introduced minimum wages might be overrepresented with respect to their sector effects: at the beginning of the observation period, minimum wage differences unequal to zero can be associated with only two or three occupations. Keeping in mind that the evidence suggests varying effects by sectors, their specific characteristics might drive the estimate, especially since a positive minimum wage effect has been observed in the largest groups (cf. fig. 2, tab. 10). Furthermore, the number of non-zero differences is smaller at the beginning of the observation period. Both aspects possibly yield the mostly insignificant estimates on three-period lagged minimum wage differences. For one more reason, a sector-specific analysis is helpful to rule out these imprecisions.

Previous literature on educational effects of minimum wages and on educational success in general, lays stress on the heredity of education (cf. Constant/Zimmermann, 2003; Modesto, 2003) Hence, the lack of an adequate control variable for an individual's family background is a shortcoming here. Although the family situation is captured by FE or by person-specific intercepts in the MIL model (cf. Rabe-Hesketh/Skrondal, 2005, pp. 116-117), relying on a concrete estimate would be preferable in order to determine the actual size of the impact. Thus, future investigation will be enriched by a respective control variable.

Finally, the evidence on sectoral wage floor effects has been used here to judge the youth exceptions concerning the statutory, nation-wide minimum wage. Basically, it appears reasonable to assume that the initiator of a minimum wage is irrelevant for economic behavior: if a firm has to reoptimize labor demand, it makes the same decisions regardless of whether the wage floor is given by a CBA or by the government. However, the overall economic consequences might differ. In contrast to sectoral wage floors, the general minimum wage is equal to all workers and is not adjusted to occupational or regional features. Thus, its scope and the degrees of affection are likely to be different.

The same line of argumentation can be followed for the educational decisions of youths. Although they probably do not depend on whether the minimum wage is sectoral or general, the universality of a wage floor might induce other changes in occupational preferences. Moreover, regarding further analysis, a general minimum wage allows for an easier representation of students which is not possible here. The method used in this thesis requires information on both the educational activity and the occupation of an individual in order to associate a sectoral minimum wage. With a general minimum, all individuals are applicable, regardless of their occupations or fields of study. Thus, the minimum wage value is not missing for students and its influence on a full set of educational alternatives can be analyzed. Evidently, this extension helps to precise the investigation of educational motives. Regarding these potential improvements, the need for deeper research in the future is clearly demonstrated.

7 Conclusion

The research purpose of this master thesis was to reveal the impact of minimum wage regulations on educational incentives of youths in Germany. This question is mainly interesting in light of the ongoing discussion about minimum wage effects which has been launched by the introduction of the first statutory wage floor in Germany at the beginning of 2015. Critics have been raising concerns over potentially negative impacts for young employees in case of minimum applicability: beside a reduction in employment, they argue that youths feel discouraged from professional education but prefer an entry into an unskilled full-time employment. Addressing this issue, the German government has decided to exempt the under-aged, professionally unskilled youth as well as apprentices from the statutory wage floor.

Section 2 provided a general overview of educational effects of minimum wages. The underlying theoretical considerations, based on the Human Capital Theory, suggest a negative impact arising from higher opportunity costs of education caused by the newly attainable wage minimum. This outcome is stated the Queuing Hypothesis. Thus, the basic theory confirms the critics concerns. However, wage floors also induce an employers' reaction in terms of a declining demand for less qualified workers replacing them by high-skilled workers which is referred to as the Substitution Hypothesis. Thus, the accumulation of skills is stimulated by lower career prospects without professional education. The evidence found in previous studies confirms negative educational effects. Particularly in Anglo-American regions, youths are discouraged from completing school and search for an employment. Furthermore, the importance of country-specific labor market policies and characteristics has been scrutinized. The results point at different minimum wage effects on highly activating and protective labor markets like in Germany, compared to deregulated ones, for instance in the U.S.

As the German statutory minimum wage has been in use for less than one year, no data base is available to carry out an empirical analysis. However, the German history of minimum wages provides an alternative discussed in section 3: in 1997, the MLSA declared the first sectoral CBA made by representants of trade unions and employers' associations generally binding and thereby introduced a sectoral wage floor. Their use has been common ever since then, yet it is decreasing up to the present. Thus, sectoral minima are used to empirically determine whether they negatively influence the educational decisions of school-leavers.

In section 4, the empirical framework was presented. Extending the methods from previous studies, a panel regression model estimating the effect of absolute and relative minimum wage differences on the binary choice regarding professional education is specified. Beside a linear GLS approach and a CL model which has been a standard approach before, a MIL model is applied which addresses several data issues such as heteroskedasticity, autocorrelation over time and a violation of IIA. For a sample of youths aged 17 to 24 and not qualified for university, the probability of choosing an apprenticeship training rather than an unskilled employment is estimated, depending on the changes in minimum wage levels and several control variables. The respective data, covering the years 1994 to 2013, is mainly taken from the GSOEP to which the official levels of sectoral wage floors and information on the labor market situation are added.

Section 5 displayed the results obtained: the impact is positive and significantly different from zero, indicating that a sectoral minimum wage encourages youths to undergo further education. Though, the actual effect is small in size. The mean probability to choose an apprenticeship is about 0.8 which signifies a generally large preference for professional education. Depending on the length of lags, relative minimum wage rises increase this probability by about 0.3 percentage points on average. Moreover, personal characteristics, such as gender and school degrees, are significantly influential on the apprenticeship probability. The results have been checked in several sensitivity tests and are shown to be stable in general. Nevertheless, the evidence suggested to re-estimate the effects on a lower sectoral level as the specific features appear to imply substantial explanatory power concerning the choice of professional education. In particular, youths adapt to the skill requirements to carry out a specific occupation.

Interpreting the evidence in section 6, the educational stimulation is characterized as a reaction of youths to a minimum wage shift in labor demand. Since the employment prospects of low-skilled workers worsen in the course of a wage floor, obtaining professional qualifications ensures future employability of school-leavers, especially in sectors with high education standards. Thus, the Substitution Hypothesis applies to the German labor market. The positive effect on further skill acquisition is boosted by the German apprenticeship system that allows for work and training at the same time. Furthermore, from the generally high educational disposition and the significant impact of non-economic characteristics, it can be concluded that economic aspects such as attainable wages are secondary to educational norms and personal properties. Although, the supposed negative effects on education are not observed here, the youth exemptions from the statutory minimum wage can be judged as reasonable: they ensure that both incentives and opportunities for school-leavers are unchanged with regard to professional education. However to take full effect, they should entirely cover the youth. The existing exemption exhibits a too low age limit that does not refer to the actual group of educational decision-makers. Finally, the need for future investigation has been outlined. Beside including further adequate control variables, e. g. for an individual's family background, a sector-specific analysis helps to examine potentially contrasting educational effects of minimum wages according to sectoral skill requirements.

References

Acemoglu, D. & Pischke, J.-S. (1998). Why Do Firms Train? Theory and Evidence. *Quarterly Journal of Economics, 113*(1), 79–119.

Agell, J. & Lommerud, K. E. (1997). Minimum wages and the incentives for skill formation. *Journal of Public Economics, 64*(1), 25–40.

Allison, P. D. (2009). *Fixed Effects Regression Models.* Thousand Oaks: Sage Publications.

Amlinger, M., Bispinck, R., & Schulten, T. (2014). Jugend ohne Mindestlohn? Zur Diskussion um Ausnahme- und Sonderregelungen fur junge Beschäftigte. *WSI Report, 14.*

Antòn, J.-I. & Muñoz de Bustillo, R. (2011). The impact of the minimum wage on Spanish youth: Evidence from a natural experiment. *MPRA Paper, 33488.*

Antonczyk, D., Fitzenberger, B., & Sommerfeld, K. (2010). Rising wage inequality, the decline of collective bargaining, and the gender wage gap. *Labor Economics, 17*(5), 835–847.

Baetschmann, G., Staub, K. E., & Winkelmann, R. (2015). Consistent estimation of the fixed effects ordered logit model. *Journal of the Royal Statistical Society, Series A, 178*(3), 685–703.

Bauer, T. K., Kluve, J., Schaffner, S., & Schmidt, C. M. (2009). Fiscal Effects of Minimum Wages - An Analysis for Germany. *German Economic Review, 10*(2), 224–242.

Becker, G. S. (1964). *Human Capital: A Theoretical and Empirical Analysis, With Special Reference To Education.* New York: National Bureau of Economic Research.

Boockmann, B., Krumm, R., Neumann, M., & Rattenhuber, P. (2013). Turning the Switch: An Evaluation of the Minimum Wage in the German Electrical Trade Using Repeated Natural Experiments. *German Economic Review, 14*(3), 316–348.

Borooah, V. K. (2002). *Logit and Probit: Ordered and Multinomial Models.* Thousand Oaks: Sage Publications.

Büchel, F. (2002). Successful apprenticeship-to-work transitions: On the long-term change in significance of the German school-leaving certificate. *International Journal of Manpower, 23*(5), 394–410.

Cahuc, P. & Zylberberg, A. (2004). *Labor Economics.* Cambridge: MIT Press.

Campolieti, M., Fang, T., & Gunderson, M. (2005). How Minimum Wages Affect Schooling-Employment Outcomes in Canada, 1993-1999. *Journal of Labor Research, 26*(3), 533–545.

Chaplin, D. D., Turner, M. D., & Pape, A. D. (2003). Minimum wages and school enrollment of teenagers: a look at the 1990's. *Economics of Education Review, 22*(1), 11–21.

Checchi, D. (2006). *The Economics of Education: Human Capital, Family Background and Inequality.* Cambridge: Cambridge University Press.

Confederation of German Employers' Associations. (2014). Position to the Introduction of a Statutory Minimum Wage. Retrieved December 17, 2015, from http://www.arbeitgeber.de/www/arbeitgeber.nsf/res/kompakt-Gesetzlicher-Mindestlohn.pdf/%5C$file/kompakt-Gesetzlicher-Mindestlohn.pdf

Constant, A. & Zimmermann, K. F. (2003). Occupational Choice Across Generations. *IZA Discussion Paper, 975.*

Currie, J. & Fallick, B. C. (1996). The Minimum Wage and the Employment of Youth: Evidence from the NYSL. *Journal of Human Resources, 31*(2), 404–428.

Dustmann, C. (2004). Parental background, secondary school track choice, and wages. *Oxford Economic Papers, 56*(2), 209–230.

Dustmann, C., Ludsteck, J., & Schönberg, U. (2009). Revisiting the German Wage Structure. *Quarterly Journal of Economics, 124*(2), 843–881.

Ehrenberg, R. G. & Marcus, A. J. (1982). Minimum Wages and Teenagers' Enrollment-Employment Outcomes: A Multinomial Logit Model. *Journal of Human Resources, 17*(1), 39–58.

Eichhorst, W. & Marx, P. (2011). Reforming German labour market institutions: A dual path to flexibility. *Journal of European Social Policy, 21*(1), 73–87.

European Council. (1998). Council Regulation (EC) No 2866/98 of 31 December 1998 on the conversion rates between the euro and the currencies of the Member States adopting the euro. Retrieved December 17, 2015, from http://eur-lex.europa.eu/legal-content/EN/TXT/PDF/?uri=CELEX:31998R2866&from=EN

European Council. (2006). Regulation (EC) No 1893/2006 of the European Parliament and of the Council of 20 December 2006 establishing the statistical classification of economic activities NACE Revision 2 and amending Council Regulation (EEC) No 3037/90 as well as certain EC Regulations on specific statistical domains. Retrieved December 17, 2015, from http://eur-lex.europa.eu/legal-content/EN/TXT/PDF/?uri=CELEX:32006R1893&from=EN

Federal Ministry of Labor and Social Affairs. (2015a). Information Figure on Minimum Wage Exceptions. Retrieved December 17, 2015, from http://www.der-mindestlohn-wirkt.de/SharedDocs/Downloads/ml/Infografiken/infografik-mindestlohn-ausnahmen.pdf?__blob=publicationFile

Federal Ministry of Labor and Social Affairs. (2015b). Register of Generally Binding Collective Bargaining Agreements. Retrieved December 17, 2015, from https://www.bmas.de/SharedDocs/Downloads/DE/PDF-Publikationen-DinA4/arbeitsrecht-verzeichnis-allgemeinverbindlicher-tarifvertraege.pdf?__blob=publicationFile

Federal Statistical Office. (1992). *Klassifikation der Berufe 1992 (KldB 92).* Retrieved December 17, 2015, from https://www.destatis.de/DE/Methoden/Klassifikationen/Berufe/KlassifikationKldb92.html

Federal Statistical Office. (2015). Genesis-online Database. Retrieved December 17, 2015, from https://www-genesis.destatis.de/genesis/online/logon

Fitzenberger, B., Kohn, K., & Wang, Q. (2011). The erosion of union membership in Germany: determinants, densities, decompositions. *Journal of Population Economics, 24*(1), 141–165.

Franz, W. & Soskice, D. W. (1995). The German apprenticeship system. In F. Buttler, W. Franz, R. Schettkat, & D. W. Soskice (Eds.), *Institutional Frameworks and Labor Market Performance: Comparative views on the U.S. and German economies* (pp. 208–234). London: Routledge.

Frick, J. & Haisken-DeNew, J. (2005). *Desktop Companion to the German Socio-Economic Panel (SOEP).* Berlin.

Frings, H. (2013). The Employment Effect of Industry-Specific, Collectively Bargained Minimum Wages. *German Economic Review, 14*(3), 258–281.

German Green Party. (2013). Federal Election Program 2013. Retrieved September 1, 2015, from https://www.gruene.de/fileadmin/user_upload/Dokumente/Gruenes-Bundestagswahlprogramm-2013.pdf#page=88

German Social Democratic Party. (2015). Position to the Introduction of a Statutory Minimum Wage. Retrieved September 1, 2015, from http://www.spdfraktion.de/themen/mindestlohn

German Socio-Economic Panel. (2015). Data for years 1984-2013, version 30.

German Trade Newspaper. (2015). Criticism of the Documentary Obligation of the Statutory Minimum Wage. Retrieved November 18, 2015, from http://www.handwerks blatt.de/handwerk/mindestlohn-handwerk-gegen-buerokratie-23479.html

German Trade Union Confederation. (2015). Arguments in Favor of a Statutory Minimum Wage. Retrieved December 17, 2015, from http://www.dgb.de/schwerpunkt/mindestlohn/hintergrund/argumente

Goebel, J. (2014a). *SOEP Documentation Codebook v29: Generated Variables in the $PEQUIV Files – Personal Level.* Retrieved December 17, 2015, from http://www.diw.de/en/diw%5C_02.c.239921.en/codebooks.html

Goebel, J. (2014b). *SOEP Documentation Codebook v29: Generated Variables – Personal Level.* Retrieved December 17, 2015, from http://www.diw.de/en/diw%5C_02.c.239921.en/codebooks.html

Goebel, J. (2014c). *SOEP Documentation Codebook v29: Person Level Questionnaires.* Retrieved December 17, 2015, from http://www.diw.de/en/diw%5C_02.c.239921.en/codebooks.html

Greene, W. H. (2012). *Econometric Analysis* (7th ed.). Upper Saddle River: Pearson Education International.

Hensher, D. A. & Greene, W. H. (2003). The Mixed Logit model: The state of practice. *Transportation, 30*(2), 133–176.

Hyslop, D. & Stillman, S. (2007). Youth minimum wage reform and the labor market in New Zealand. *Labor Economics, 14*(2), 201–230.

Institute of Economic and Social Research. (2015). Tariff Commitment in Germany 1998-2014. Retrieved December 17, 2015, from http://www.boeckler.de/wsi-tarifarchiv%5C_2257.htm

Knaab, A. & Schöb, R. (2008). Minimum Wage Incidence: The Case for Germany. *CESifo Working Paper, 2432.*

Landon, S. (1997). High School Enrollment, Minimum Wages and Education Spending. *Canadian Public Policy, 23*(2), 141–163.

Mincer, J. A. (1974). *Schooling, Experience and Earnings.* New York: Columbia University Press.

Mincer, J. A. & Leighton, L. (1980). Effect of Minimum Wages on Human Capital Formation. *NBER Working Paper, 441.*

Modesto, L. (2003). Should I stay or should I go? Educational choices and earnings: An empirical study for Portugal. *Journal of Population Economics, 16*(2), 307–322.

Möller, J. (2012). Minimum wages in German industries – what does the evidence tell us so far? *Journal of Labor Market Research, 45*(3), 187–199.

Möller, J. (2014). Werden die Auswirkungen des Mindestlohns überschätzt? ZBW Zeitgespräch. *Wirtschaftsdienst 2014.*

Müller, K.-U. & Steiner, V. (2009). Would a Legal Minimum Wage Reduce Poverty? A Micro-simulation Study for Germany. *Journal of Income Distribution, 18*(3-4), 131–151.

Neumark, D. & Wascher, W. (1995a). Minimum Wage Effects on Employment and School Enrollment. *Journal of Business & Economic Statistics, 13*(2), 199–206.

Neumark, D. & Wascher, W. (1995b). Minimum-Wage Effects on School and Work Transitions of Teenagers. *American Economic Review, 85*(2), 244–249.

Neumark, D. & Wascher, W. (2003). Minimum wages and skill acquisition: another look at schooling effects. *Economics of Education Review, 22*(1), 1–10.

Neumark, D. & Wascher, W. (2004). Minimum Wages , Labor Market Institutions, and Youth Employment: A Cross-National Analysis. *Industrial and Labor Relations Review, 57*(2), 223–248.

Neumark, D. & Wascher, W. (2010). *Minimum Wages.* Cambridge: MIT Press.

Organization for Economic Cooperation and Development. (2015a). Indicators of Active Labor Market Policies and Activation Strategies. Retrieved December 17, 2015, from http://www.oecd.org/employment/activelabourmarketpoliciesandactivationstrategies.htm

Organization for Economic Cooperation and Development. (2015b). Indicators of Employment Protection. Retrieved December 17, 2015, from http://www.oecd.org/employment/emp/oecdindicatorsofemploymentprotection.htm

Organization for Economic Cooperation and Development. (2015c). Trade union density statistics. Retrieved December 17, 2015, from https://stats.oecd.org/Index.aspx?DataSetCode=UN_DEN

Pacheco, G. A. & Cruickshank, A. A. (2007). Minimum wage effects on educational enrollments in New Zealand. *Economics of Education Review, 26*(5), 574–587.

Palier, B. & Thelen, K. (2010). Institutionalizing Dualism: Complementarities and Change in France and Germany. *Politics & Society, 38*(1), 119–148.

Rabe-Hesketh, S. & Skrondal, A. (2005). *Multilevel and longitudinal modeling using Stata.* College Station: Stata Press.

Rattenhuber, P. (2014). Building the minimum wage: the distributional impact of Germany's first sectoral minimum wage on wages and hours across different wage bargaining regimes. *Empirical Economics, 46*(4), 1429–1446.

Revelt, D. & Train, K. (1998). Mixed Logit with Repeated Choices: Households' Choices of Appliance Efficiency Level. *The Review of Economics and Statistics, 80*(4), 647–657.

Rice, P. (2010). Minimum Wages and Schooling: Evidence from the UK's Introduction of a National Minimum Wage. *SERC Discussion Paper, 50.*

Riphahn, R. T. (2002). Residential Location and Youth Unemployment: The Economic Geography of School-to-Work Transistions. *Journal of Population Economics, 15*(1), 115–135.

Schulten, T. & Horn, G. (2014). Das Mindestlohngesetz - ein wichtiges Instrument zur Stabilisierung der Lohnentwicklung: ZBW Zeitgespräch. *Wirtschaftsdienst 2014.*

Schultz, T. W. (1981). *Investing in People: The Economics of Population Quality.* Berkeley: University of California Press.

UNESCO Institute for Statistics. (2012). *International Standard Classification of Education ISCED 2011.* Montreal.

Wooldridge, J. M. (2010). *Econometric Analysis of Cross-Section and Panel Data* (2nd ed.). Cambridge: MIT Press.

Laws Directory

This directory consists of the laws and regulations cited all of which refer to the Federal Republic of Germany.

Collective Bargaining Agreement Act, applicable as from August 25, 1969.

Federal Training Assistance Act, applicable as from August 26, 1971.

Minimum Wage Law, applicable as from January 1, 2015.

Notice on the Declaration of General Application of a Collective Bargaining Agreement in Chimney Sweep Trades, applicable as from April 30, 2014.

Notice on the Declaration of General Application of a Collective Bargaining Agreement in Electrical Trades, applicable as from June 1, 1997, inapplicable as from May 31, 1998.

Second Notice on the Declaration of General Application of a Collective Bargaining Agreement in Electrical Trades, applicable as from June 1, 1998, inapplicable as from August 31, 1999.

Third Notice on the Declaration of General Application of a Collective Bargaining Agreement in Electrical Trades, applicable as from September 1, 1999, inapplicable as from August 31, 2001.

Fourth Notice on the Declaration of General Application of a Collective Bargaining Agreement in Electrical Trades, applicable as from September 1, 2001, inapplicable as from April 30, 2003.

Fifth Notice on the Declaration of General Application of a Collective Bargaining Agreement in Electrical Trades, applicable as from September 1, 2007, inapplicable as from December 31, 2010.

Sixth Notice on the Declaration of General Application of a Collective Bargaining Agreement in Electrical Trades, applicable as from January 1, 2011, inapplicable as from December 31, 2013.

Seventh Notice on the Declaration of General Application of a Collective Bargaining Agreement in Electrical Trades, applicable as from January 1, 2014, inapplicable as from December 31, 2015.

Posted Workers Act, applicable as from April 20, 2009.

Regulation on Minimum Working Conditions in Agriculture, Gardening and Forestry, applicable as from January 1, 2015.

Regulation on Minimum Working Conditions in Barbering, applicable as from January 1, 2015, inapplicable as from July 31, 2015.

Regulation on Minimum Working Conditions in Building Cleaning, applicable as from March 1, 2008, inapplicable as from September 30, 2009.

Second Regulation on Minimum Working Conditions in Building Cleaning, applicable as from March 10, 2010, inapplicable as from December 31, 2011.

Third Regulation on Minimum Working Conditions in Building Cleaning, applicable as from January 1, 2012, inapplicable as from October 31, 2013.

Fourth Regulation on Minimum Working Conditions in Building Cleaning, applicable as from November 1, 2013, inapplicable as from October 31, 2015, replaced as from January 1, 2015.

Fifth Regulation on Minimum Working Conditions in Building Cleaning, applicable as from January 1, 2015, inapplicable as from December 31, 2015

Regulation on Minimum Working Conditions in Butchery, applicable as from August 1, 2014, inapplicable as from December 31, 2017.

Regulation on Minimum Working Conditions in Care Nursing, applicable as from August 1, 2010, inapplicable as from December 31, 2014.

Second Regulation on Minimum Working Conditions in Care Nursing, applicable as from January 1, 2015, inapplicable as from October 31, 2017.

Regulation on Minimum Working Conditions in Hard Coal Mining, applicable as from October 22, 2009, inapplicable as from October 31, 2010.

Second Regulation on Minimum Working Conditions in Hard Coal Mining, applicable as from November 1, 2011, inapplicable as from March 31, 2013.

Third Regulation on Minimum Working Conditions in Hard Coal Mining, applicable as from December 1, 2013, inapplicable as from March 31, 2015.

Regulation on Minimum Working Conditions in Laundry Services, applicable as from October 24, 2009, inapplicable as from March 31, 2013.

Second Regulation on Minimum Working Conditions in Laundry Services, applicable as from February 1, 2014, inapplicable as from September 30, 2017.

Regulation on Minimum Working Conditions in Main Construction Trades, applicable as from September 1, 1999, inapplicable as from August 31, 2000.

Second Regulation on Minimum Working Conditions in Main Construction Trades, applicable as from September 1, 2000, inapplicable as from August 31, 2002.

Third Regulation on Minimum Working Conditions in Main Construction Trades, applicable as from September 1, 2002, inapplicable as from August 31, 2004, replaced as from November 1, 2003.

Fourth Regulation on Minimum Working Conditions in Main Construction Trades, applicable as from November 1, 2003, inapplicable as from August 31, 2006, replaced as from September 1, 2005.

Fifth Regulation on Minimum Working Conditions in Main Construction Trades, applicable as from September 1, 2005, inapplicable as from August 31, 2008.

Sixth Regulation on Minimum Working Conditions in Main Construction Trades, applicable as from September 1, 2008, inapplicable as from August 31, 2009.

Seventh Regulation on Minimum Working Conditions in Main Construction Trades, applicable as from September 1, 2009, inapplicable as from November 30, 2011.

Eighth Regulation on Minimum Working Conditions in Main Construction Trades, applicable as from December 1, 2011, inapplicable as from December 31, 2013.

Ninth Regulation on Minimum Working Conditions in Main Construction Trades, applicable as from January 1, 2014, inapplicable as from December 31, 2017.

Regulation on Minimum Working Conditions in Painting & Varnishing, applicable as from March 1, 2003, inapplicable as from March 30, 2004.

Second Regulation on Minimum Working Conditions in Painting & Varnishing, applicable as from June 1, 2004, inapplicable as from September 30, 2005.

Third Regulation on Minimum Working Conditions in Painting & Varnishing, applicable as from October 1, 2005, inapplicable as from March 31, 2008.

Fourth Regulation on Minimum Working Conditions in Painting & Varnishing, applicable as from April 1, 2008, inapplicable as from June 30, 2009.

Fifth Regulation on Minimum Working Conditions in Painting & Varnishing, applicable as from August 11, 2009, inapplicable as from February 29,2012.

Sixth Regulation on Minimum Working Conditions in Painting & Varnishing, applicable as from June 1, 2012, inapplicable as from April 30, 2013.

Seventh Regulation on Minimum Working Conditions in Painting & Varnishing, applicable as from May 1, 2013, inapplicable as from April 30, 2014.

Eighth Regulation on Minimum Working Conditions in Painting & Varnishing, applicable as from August 1, 2014, inapplicable as from April 30, 2017.

Regulation on Minimum Working Conditions in Postal Services, applicable as from January 1, 2008, inapplicable as from April 30, 2010.

Regulation on Minimum Working Conditions in Professional Education, applicable as from August 1, 2012, inapplicable as from June 30, 2013.

Second Regulation on Minimum Working Conditions in Professional Education, applicable as from July 1, 2013, inapplicable as from December 31, 2015.

Regulation on Minimum Working Conditions in Roofing, applicable as from September 1, 2001, inapplicable as from August 31, 2002.

Second Regulation on Minimum Working Conditions in Roofing, applicable as from March 1, 2003, inapplicable as from December 31, 2003.

Third Regulation on Minimum Working Conditions in Roofing, applicable as from June 1, 2004, inapplicable as from December 31, 2006.

Fourth Regulation on Minimum Working Conditions in Roofing, applicable as from January 1, 2007, inapplicable as from December 31, 2009.

Fifth Regulation on Minimum Working Conditions in Roofing, applicable as from March 19, 2010, inapplicable as from December 31, 2011.

Sixth Regulation on Minimum Working Conditions in Roofing, applicable as from January 1, 2012, inapplicable as from December 31, 2013.

Seventh Regulation on Minimum Working Conditions in Roofing, applicable as from January 1 ,2014, inapplicable as from December 31, 2015.

Regulation on Minimum Working Conditions in Scaffolding, applicable as from August 1, 2013, inapplicable as from February 28, 2014.

Second Regulation on Minimum Working Conditions in Scaffolding, applicable as from September 1, 2014, inapplicable as from March 31, 2016.

Regulation on Minimum Working Conditions in Security Services, applicable as from June 1, 2011, inapplicable as from December 31, 2013.

Regulation on Minimum Working Conditions in Stone Cutting, applicable as from October 1, 2013, inapplicable as from April 30, 2015.

Regulation on Minimum Working Conditions in Subcontracted Work, applicable as from January 1, 2012, inapplicable as from October 31, 2013.

Regulation on Minimum Working Conditions in Textile Industry, applicable as from January 1, 2015, inapplicable as from December 31, 2017.

Regulation on Minimum Working Conditions in Waste Management, applicable as from December 19, 2009, inapplicable as from October 31, 2010.

Second Regulation on Minimum Working Conditions in Waste Management, applicable as from January 1, 2011, inapplicable as from August 31, 2011.

Third Regulation on Minimum Working Conditions in Waste Management, applicable as from November 1, 2011, inapplicable as from March 31, 2012.

Fourth Regulation on Minimum Working Conditions in Waste Management, applicable as from June 1, 2012, inapplicable as from December 31, 2012.

Fifth Regulation on Minimum Working Conditions in Waste Management, applicable as from February 1, 2013, inapplicable as from June 30, 2014.

Sixth Regulation on Minimum Working Conditions in Waste Management, applicable as from October 1, 2014, inapplicable as from June 30, 2015.

Vocational Training Act, applicable as from March 23, 2005.

A Literature Overview

Table A.1: Empirical Evidence of Educational and Employment Effects of Minimum Wages

Study	Country	Time Period	Regression Model	Dep. Variable	Employment Effect	Educational Effect
Mincer/Leighton (1980)	USA	1967-1971	OLS	Wage Growth, Job Tenure, Job Training Received? (y/n)	Not Observed	Negative
Ehrenberg/Marcus (1982)	USA	1966/1968	CL	Enrollment-Employment Status	Negative for Certain Groups	Negative for Certain Groups
Neumark/Wascher (1995a)	USA	1977-1989	CL	Enrollment-Employment Status	Negative	Negative
Neumark/Wascher (1995b)	USA	1979-1992	CL	Enrollment-Employment Status, Transition Probability	Negative	Negative
Currie/Fallick (1996)	USA	1979-1987	Panel OLS	Employed? (y/n)	Negative	Not Observed
Chaplin u. a. (2003)	USA	1989-1996	Panel OLS	Student Continuation Ratio	Not Observed	Negative
Neumark/Wascher (2003)	USA	1980-1998	CL	Enrollment-Employment Status	Negative	Negative
Neumark/Wascher (2004)	OECD	Not Uniform	Panel OLS, GMM	Youth Employment Rate	Depending on Labor Market Characteristics	Not Observed
Landon (1997)	Canada	1975-1989	Panel OLS	Enrollment Rate	Negative	Negative
Campolieti u. a. (2005)	Canada	1993-1999	CL	Enrollment-Employment Status	Negative	None
Hyslop/Stillman (2007)	New Zealand	1997-2003	Panel OLS	Employed? (y/n), Student? (y/n) a. o.	Negative	Negative
Pacheco/Cruickshank (2007)	New Zealand	1986-2004	Panel OLS	Enrollment Rate	Not Observed	Negative
Rice (2010)	UK	1998-1999	CL	Student? (y/n)	Not Observed	Negative
Antón/Muñoz de Bustillo (2011)	Spain	1995-1998	Linear Probability, Probit, Logit	Employed? (y/n), Student? (y/n)	Negative	Negative

Source: author's illustration

B Further Data Description

B.1 Dataset Codebook

The following glossary lists the variables used in the analyses and supporting variables taken from the GSOEP to create the regression variables. Each entry provides the variable's name, its label, an information on whether the variable was taken originally from the GSOEP[45], from the FSO or is a GSOEP-based creation by the author for the purpose of this thesis (AC = Author's Creation) and a description of manifestations. The information on GSOEP variables is taken from Goebel (2014a,b,c).

Variables directly or indirectly used in the regression analysis:

`year` *Survey Year* (GSOEP), year under observation. Limited to values between 1994 and 2013.

`educ_stat_youth` *Educational Status* (AC), captures the educational or occupational alternatives for school-leavers without higher secondary degrees, i. e. *Working Unskilled* (0) and *Doing an Apprenticeship* (1). Refers to persons aged 17 to 24, excluding students at schools and universities as well as individuals doing a civil or military service (these are not considered occupational alternatives).

`isced` *ISCED Level* (GSOEP), gives the highest educational level of an individual based on the ISCED scale. Distinguishes between *Still in School* (0), *No Approved Schooling* (1), *General Elementary Education* (2), *Middle Vocational Education* (3), *Vocational Education + Abitur* (4), *Higher Vocational Education* (5) and *Academic Education* (6). Level 3 comprises of either a higher secondary degree **or** a voca-

[45] The respective variables are not self-created, however, they are usually renamed, relabelled and/or recoded for consistency reasons.

tional training. Level 4 comprises of a higher secondary degree **and** a vocational training. Level 5 comprises of higher vocational degrees, e. g. German *Meister*. Level 6 comprises of all kinds of academic education.

`isced_alt` *ISCED Level (modified)* (AC), corresponds to `isced` but excludes persons still in school and the academic track. Distinguishes between *No Approved Schooling* (1), *General Elementary Education* (2), *Middle Vocational Education* (3), *Vocational Education + Abitur* (4) and *Higher Vocational Education* (5). Descriptions of the single levels are as for `isced`.

`minwage_stat` *Minimum Wage in Occupational Group* (AC), gives the gross hourly generally binding sectoral minimum wage in € for an individual's profession valid on January 1 of the respective year under observation. The information on general binding minimum wages is taken from the official regulations (see Laws Directory). The association of individuals and minimum wages is based on the comparison of professions applicable for a minimum wage according to the legislations and professions indicated by survey respondents, following the FSO-1992-Classification of occupations.

`diff_minwage_stat` *(Δ Minimum Wage)$_t$* (AC), gives the first difference of `minwage_stat`.

`diff_minwage_statl1` *(Δ Minimum Wage)$_{t-1}$* (AC), gives the one-period lagged value of `diff_minwage_stat`.

`diff_minwage_statl2` *(Δ Minimum Wage)$_{t-2}$* (AC), gives the two-period lagged value of `diff_minwage_stat`.

`diff_minwage_statl3` *(Δ Minimum Wage)$_{t-3}$* (AC), gives the three-period lagged value of `diff_minwage_stat`.

`medianw_state` *State Median Wage* (AC), gives the median of gross hourly wages in € on federal state level. Represents all workers' wages including part-time and marginally employed persons and apprentices. The information on wages and federal states of residence are taken from `wage_gro` and `fed_state`.

`diff_medianw_state` *(Δ State Median Wage)$_t$* (AC), gives the first difference of `medianw_state`.

`diff_medianw_statel1` *(Δ State Median Wage)$_{t-1}$* (AC), gives the one-period lagged value of `diff_medianw_state`.

`diff_medianw_statel2` *(Δ State Median Wage)$_{t-2}$* (AC), gives the two-period lagged value of `diff_medianw_state`.

`diff_medianw_statel3` *(Δ State Median Wage)$_{t-3}$* (AC), gives the three-period lagged value of `diff_medianw_state`.

`kaitz_stat_reg` *Kaitz Index* (AC), displays the ratio of the minimum wage an individual is eligible for to the median wage in the individual's state of residence. Computed as `minwage_stat` divided by `medianw_state`.

`diff_kaitz` *(Δ Kaitz Index)$_t$* (AC), gives the first difference of `kaitz_stat_reg`.

`diff_kaitzl1` *(Δ Kaitz Index)$_{t-1}$* (AC), gives the one-period lagged value of `diff_kaitz`.

`diff_kaitzl2` *(Δ Kaitz Index)$_{t-2}$* (AC), gives the two-period lagged value of `diff_kaitz`.

`diff_kaitzl3` *(Δ Kaitz Index)$_{t-3}$* (AC), gives the three-period lagged value of `diff_kaitz`.

`mw_exist` *Minimum Wage Existence$_t$* (AC), indicator variable, captures the applicability (1) or non-applicability (0) of an individual for a generally binding sectoral minimum wage.

`mw_existl1` *Minimum Wage Existence$_{t-1}$* (AC), gives the one-period lagged value of `mw_exist`.

mw_existl2 *Minimum Wage Existence*$_{t-2}$ (AC), gives the two-period lagged value of mw_exist.

mw_existl3 *Minimum Wage Existence*$_{t-3}$ (AC), gives the three-period lagged value of mw_exist.

sex *Sex* (GSOEP), indicator capturing whether a person is male (0) or female (1).

natio *Nationality* (GSOEP), indicator capturing whether a person is German (0) or Non-German (1).

age *Age* (AC), gives an individual's age in years. Calculated as the difference between year and birth_year.

age_group *Age Group* (AC), indicates whether an individual belongs to the youth group of 17- to 24-year-olds (1) or to the adult group (0).

schooldeg *Secondary School Degree* (GSOEP), gives the secondary school degree obtained by an individual: No Degree (0), Still in School (1), Lower Degree (2), Medium Degree or Other Degree (3), Fachabitur (4), Abitur (5).

schooldeg_sec *Lower to Medium Secondary School Degree* (AC), gives the secondary school degree obtained by an individual excluding higher secondary degrees and students: No Degree (0), Lower Degree (1), Medium Degree or Other Degree (2).

abi *Indicator of Higher Secondary Degree* (AC), indicates whether an individual has obtained the German Fachabitur or Abitur (1) or not (0). Based on schooldeg.

educ_necessary *Required Education for Occupation* (GSOEP), gives the level of education that is necessary to carry out an individual's current occupation: *No Professional Training Necessary* (1), *Orientation* (2), *Introduction* (3), *Course Training* (4), *Professional Training* (5), *Academic Training* (6).

uer_reg *State Unemployment Rate* (FSO), gives the percentage rate of registered unemployed persons with respect to civil employees on federal state level. Only available for the years 1991 to 2013.

diff_uer_reg *(Δ State Unemployment Rate)$_t$* (FSO), gives the first difference of **uer_reg**.

diff_uer_regl1 *(Δ State Unemployment Rate)$_{t-1}$* (FSO), gives the one-period lagged values of **diff_uer_reg**.

diff_uer_regl4 *(Δ State Unemployment Rate)$_{t-4}$* (FSO), gives the four-period lagged values of **diff_uer_reg**.

appren_place *Number of Apprenticeship Places* (FSO), gives the number of officially registered apprenticeship places in thousands, both occupied and non-occupied, on September 1 of the year under observation.

diff_appren_place *(Δ Number of Apprenticeship Places)$_t$* (FSO), gives the first difference of appren_place.

diff_appren_placel1 *(Δ Number of Apprenticeship Places)$_{t-1}$* (FSO), gives the one-period lagged value of **diff_appren_place**.

diff_appren_placel4 *(Δ Number of Apprenticeship Places)$_{t-4}$* (FSO), gives the four-period lagged value of **diff_appren_place**.

cohortsize *Relative Youth Cohort Size* (AC), gives the relative size of the youth cohort as the ratio of the number of youths (aged 17 to 24) to the entire population, multiplied by 100.

diff_cohortsize *(Δ Relative Youth Cohort Size)$_t$* (AC), gives the first difference of cohortsize.

diff_cohortsizel1 *(Δ Relative Youth Cohort Size)$_{t-1}$* (AC), gives the one-period lagged value of **diff_cohortsize**.

`diff_cohortsizel4` *(Δ Relative Youth Cohort Size)*$_{t-4}$ (AC), gives the four-period lagged value of `diff_cohortsize`.

`hh_income` *Post-Government Household Income* (GSOEP), gives the average monthly post-government income in thousand € for the year under observation referring to the household an individual lives in. Bases on annual post-government household income divided by 1000, then divided by 12.

`diff_hh_income` *(Δ Household Income)*$_t$ (AC), gives the first difference of `hh_income`.

`diff_hh_incomel1` *(Δ Household Income)*$_{t-1}$ (AC), gives the one-period lagged value of `diff_hh_income`.

`time` *Time* (AC), continuous variable, gives the year under observation thereby allowing to control for time effects. Mostly used as a factor variable.

`sector_nace` *Economic Sector according to NACE* (GSOEP), gives the economic sector an individual works in according to the NACE classification. Takes up 100 values with different numbers of observations. Examples: Electrical Trades (40), Construction (45), Health Care System (85). See GSOEP codebook for full description. Mostly used as a factor variable.

`fed_state` *Federal State of Residence* (GSOEP), gives an individual's state of residence: Schleswig-Holstein (1), Hamburg (2), Lower Saxony (3), Bremen (4), North-Rhine-Westfalia (5), Hessen (6), Rheinland-Pfalz (7), Baden-Wuerttemberg (8), Bavaria (9), Saarland (10), Berlin (11), Brandenburg (12), Mecklenburg-Vorpommern (13), Saxony (14), Saxony-Anhalt (15),Thuringia (16).

`region` *Region of Residence* (GSOEP), indicator capturing whether an individual lives in West Germany (0) or East Germany (1).

Supportive variables used to construct regression variables:

`birth_year` *Year of Birth* (GSOEP), gives an individual's year of birth.

`stat` *Employment Status* (GSOEP), gives an individual's employment status in the year under observation: *Full-time Employed* (1), *Part-time Employed* (2), *Apprentice* (3), *Marginally Employed* (4), *Partial Retirement* (5), *Military Service* (6), *Civil Service* (7), *Sheltered Workshop* (8), *Non-working* (9), *Military or Civil Service* (16).

`occup_klas` *Occupation according to FSO-1992-Classification* (GSOEP), gives the code of an individual's current occupation following the FSO-1992-Classification of occupations. Each occupation is coded with a three- to four-digit number sorted by occupational families or economic sectors respectively. Examples: scaffolder (4430), nurse (8530), hairdresser (9010). The association of occupations with minimum wages is based on this coding.

`profdeg` *Professional Degree* (GSOEP), captures the kind of professional degree obtained if valid: vocational training (1), health care school (2), professional school, foreman school (3), civil servant training (4), other professional degree (5).

`unideg` *University Degree* (GSOEP), captures the kind of university degree obtained if valid: university of applied sciences (1), (technical) university (2), university abroad (3), school of engineering (East Germany) (4), university (East Germany) (5), doctorate or habilitation (6), doctorate abroad (7).

`noprofdeg` *No Professional Degree Obtained* (GSOEP), indicates whether an individual has obtained a professional degree (1) or not (0).

`no_profdeg_yet` *No Professional Degree Obtained So Far* (GSOEP), indicates the activity in progress for individuals without completed professional education: *No Professional Degree* (1), *Apprenticeship in Progress* (2), *University Studies in Progress* (2) `occup` *Working in Trained Occupation?* (GSOEP), captures whether an individual is carrying out an occupation once trained as: *Yes* (1), *Still in Training* (2), *No* (3), *No Professional Education Received* (4).

`activity_occup` *Current Activity = Trained Occupation?* (GSOEP), defined as `occup`.

`profeduc_now` *Vocational Training in Progress?* (GSOEP), indicates whether an individual is undergoing vocational training at the moment (1) or not (0).

`work_time` *Working Hours Per Week* (GSOEP), captures the individual amount of agreed weekly working hours.

`wage_gro` *Gross Hourly Wage in €* (AC), gives the individual gross hourly wage in €. Constructed as the gross monthly wage taken from the GSOEP divided by 4, then divided by weekly work time `work_time`.

`unemployed` *Unemployed?* (GSOEP), indicates whether an individual is unemployed (1) or not (0).

`selfemployed` *Self-Employed?* (GSOEP), indicates whether an individual is self-employed (1) or not (0).

B.2 Supplementary Descriptive Statistics

Table B.1: Summary Statistics, Full Sample, All Variables

Variable	Obs	Mean	Std. Dev.	Min	Max
Survey Year	2,090,112	2001.5	6.922	1990	2013
Educational Status	23,063	0.712	0.453	0	1
ISCED Level	436,060	3.427	1.506	0	6
ISCED Level (Modified)	36,272	2.564	0.71	1	5
Minimum Wage	1,953,792	0.052	0.688	0	12.6
State Median Wage	523,358	13.702	2.911	3.193	19.481
Kaitz Index	1,953,792	0.004	0.048	0	0.993
Existence of Minimum Wage	2,090,112	0.005	0.073	0	1
Δ Minimum Wage	1,872,384	0.008	0.587	-11.53	12.6
Δ State Median Wage	442,352	0.281	0.605	-6.981	7.513
Δ Kaitz Index	1,872,384	0.001	0.041	-0.909	0.926
Sex	576,702	0.518	0.5	0	1
Nationality	471,901	1.093	0.29	1	2
Age	572,372	38.404	22.431	0	110
Age Group	2,090,112	0.034	0.182	0	1
Year of Birth	572,526	1964.393	22.68557	1894	2013
Lower to Medium Secondary School Degree	291,916	1.429	0.577	0	2
Secondary School Degree	378,565	3.833	1.2	1	6
Professional Degree	242,697	1.665	1.144	1	5
University Degree	62,209	2.272	1.266	1	7
No Professional Degree Obtained	780	1	0	1	1
Required Education for Occupation	202,583	4.469881	1.386525	1	6
Federal State of Residence	523,358	8.112	3.958	1	16
Region of Residence	523,360	0.244	0.429	0	1
National Unemployment Rate	2,003,024	10.2	1.7	7.3	13
State Unemployment Rate	506,533	10.459	4.391	3.7	22.1
Monthly Household Income (in Thousand €)	569,650	2.983	2.219	0	234.579
Number of Apprenticeship Places (in Thousand)	1,480,496	449.471	52.17	360.016	519.554
Relative Youth Cohort Size	2,090,112	3.412	0.744	2.364	4.676
Δ National Unemployment Rate	2,003,024	0.335	1.732	-1.9	7.3
Δ State Unemployment Rate	442,352	0.261	1.892	-15.9	14.6
Δ Household Income	483,162	0.059	1.371	-223.652	157.95
Δ Number of Apprenticeship Places	1,393,408	2.708	32.111	-37.764	93.848

Table B.1: Summary Statistics, Full Sample, All Variables - Continued

Variable	Obs	Mean	Std. Dev.	Min	Max
Δ Relative Youth Cohort Size	2,003,024	0.08	0.418	-0.286	1.55
Indicator of Higher Secondary Degree	368,232	0.207	0.405	0	1
No Professional Degree Obtained So Far	109,381	1.342	0.653	1	3
Vocational Training in Progress?	386,495	0.11	0.313	0	1
Employment Status	386,503	4.851	3.811	1	16
Unemployed?	380,876	0.069	0.254	0	1
Current Activity = Trained Occupation?	132,242	1.94	1.067	1	4
Working in Trained Occupation?	207,365	1.921	1.066	1	4
Working Hours per Week	193,778	34.995	8.809	0	80
Occupation According to FSO-1992-Classification	207,042	6554.372	2229.194	110	9971
Gross Hourly Wage	193,767	14.968	10.331	0	826.25
Economic Sector According to NACE	199,827	56.728	24.091	1	100
Time	1,953,792	2001.5	6.922	1990	2013

Sources: GSOEP, FSO, minimum wage regulations; author's calculations

Table B.2: Summary Statistics, Baseline Sample, All Variables

Variable	Obs	Mean	Std. Dev.	Min	Max
Survey Year	8,062	2002.703	5.546	1994	2013
Educational Status	8,062	0.812	0.391	0	1
ISCED Level	8,062	2.073	0.516	1	6
ISCED Level (Modified)	8,042	2.064	0.478	1	5
Minimum Wage	8,062	0.942	2.779	0	11.2
State Median Wage	8,062	13.823	2.362	8.05	19.481
Kaitz Index	8,062	0.068	0.201	0	0.904
Existence of Minimum Wage	8,062	0.104	0.306	0	1
Δ Minimum Wage	8,062	0.478	2.347	-11.05	11.2
Δ State Median Wage	7,054	0.287	0.566	-3.902	7.445
Δ Kaitz Index	8,062	0.034	0.169	-0.83	0.904
Sex	8,062	0.433	0.495	0	1
Nationality	7,148	0.126	0.332	0	1
Age	8,062	20.183	1.93	17	24
Age Group	8,062	1	0	1	1
Year of Birth	8,062	1982.519	5.676	1970	1996
Lower to Medium Secondary School Degree	8,062	1.558	0.588	0	2

Table B.2: Summary Statistics, Baseline Sample, All Variables - Continued

Variable	Obs	Mean	Std. Dev.	Min	Max
Secondary School Degree	8,062	3.509	0.741	1	4
Professional Degree	933	1.477	0.928	1	5
University Degree	20	1.2	0.616	1	3
No Professional Degree Obtained	0	–	–	–	–
Required Education for Occupation	6,719	4.341569	1.189608	1	6
Federal State of Residence	8,062	8.394	3.986	1	16
Region of Residence	8,062	0.265	0.441	0	1
National Unemployment Rate	8,062	10.613	1.517	7.6	13
State Unemployment Rate	8,062	10.997	4.706	4.2	22.1
Monthly Household Income (in Thousand €)	8,062	3.014	1.903	0	48.632
Number of Apprenticeship Places (in Thousand)	6,771	449.091	50.539	360.016	519.554
Relative Youth Cohort Size	8,062	3.591	0.774	2.364	4.676
Δ National Unemployment Rate	8,062	-0.061	0.844	-1.9	1.3
Δ State Unemployment Rate	7,054	-0.041	1.2	-13.1	11.7
Δ Household Income	7,054	0.085	1.119	-16.558	24.336
Δ Number of Apprenticeship Places	6,364	-1.042	31.253	-37.764	93.848
Δ Relative Youth Cohort Size	8,062	0.176	0.514	-0.286	1.55
Indicator of Higher Secondary School Degree	8,062	0	0	0	0
No Professional Degree Obtained So Far	7,626	1.779	0.415	1	2
Vocational Training in Progress?	8,062	0.782	0.413	0	1
Employment Status	8,062	2.615	0.927	1	8
Umemployed?	8,044	0.012	0.107	0	1
Current Activity = Trained Occupation?	5,875	2.236	0.773	1	4
Working in Trained Occupation?	8,045	2.18	0.727	1	4
Working Hours per Week	7,491	37.743	5.646	1.5	60
Occupation According to FSO-1992-Classification	8,062	5,786.323	2,510.886	110	9971
Gross Hourly Wage in €	7,491	5.076	3.934	0	79.938
Economic Sector According to NACE	7,516	54.16	23.782	1	100
Time	8,062	2002.703	5.546	1994	2013

Notes: Some observations are included in the baseline sample although they already obtained a vocational degree or a university degree. They are classified as apprentices or unskilled workers because they do not work in the occupation they trained as or learn another.

Sources: GSOEP, FSO, minimum wage regulations; author's calculations

Table B.3: Percentage of Youths in Selected Occupational Activities

Activity	% of Youths Aged <18	% of Youths Aged 18-20	% of Youths Aged 21-24
Full-Time Employment	0.6	7.59	37.8
Part-Time Employment	0.1	1.40	4.13
Apprenticeship	16.74	33.01	14.28
Marginally Employed	2.69	4.48	5.45
Military or Civil Service	0.09	2.38	3.41
Sheltered Workshop	–	0.07	0.24
Not Working	79.66	51.08	34.66

Source: GSOEP; author's calculations

Table B.4: Association of Occupations with Minimum Wages

Label of Occupational Group	Codes FSO-1992-Classification	Minimum Introduction	In Baseline Sample?
Agriculture, Gardening & Forestry	100-140, 200-243, 500-529, 600-629	2015	No
Barbering	9010-9019	2013	No
Building Cleaning	9340-9343, 9349	2007	Yes
Butchery	400-4017	2014	No
Care Nursing	8640-8657	2009	Yes
Chimney Sweep Trades	8040-8042	2014	No
Electrical Trades	3100-3152, 3157-3177, 3200-3229	1997	Yes
Hard Coal Mining	700-727	2009	No[a]
Main Construction Trades	4000-4429, 4600-4889, 5440, 5446-5469	1997	Yes
Laundry Services	9300-9359	2009	Yes
Painting & Varnishing	5100-5149	2003	Yes
Postal Services	7300-7354	2007	Yes
Professional Education	8680-8682, 8769, 8855, 8856	2012	No[a]
Scaffolding	4430-4437	2013	No
Security Services	7900-7912, 7920-7929	2011	Yes
Stone Cutting	1000-1019	2013	No
Textile Industry	3400-3619, 6733	2015	No
Roofing	4880-4889	1997	No[a]
Waste Management	9350-9359	2010	Yes

Notes: [a] due to a lack of observations for the dependent variable

Sources: GSOEP, FSO, minimum wage regulations; author's calculations

Table B.5: Dickey-Fuller Test for Stationarity, Original Variables
H_0: Time Series is Instationary

Variable	Test Statistic τ	P-Value	Reject H_0?
Minimum Wage (Main Construction Trades, West)	-1.051	0.7341	No
Minimum Wage (Main Construction Trades, East)	0.520	0.9855	No
Minimum Wage (Electrical Trades, West)	-1.175	0.6842	No
Minimum Wage (Electrical Trades, East)	-0.250	0.9323	No
Minimum Wage (Painting & Varnishing, West)	-0.701	0.8464	No
Minimum Wage (Painting & Varnishing, East)	-0.414	0.9078	No
Minimum Wage (Building Cleaning, West)	-1.176	0.6840	No
Minimum Wage (Building Cleaning, East)	0.348	0.9794	No
Minimum Wage (Hard Coal Mining, West)	-0.873	0.7968	No
Minimum Wage (Hard Coal Mining, East)	0.294	0.9771	No
Minimum Wage (Waste Management, West)	2.761	1.0000	No
Minimum Wage (Waste Management, East)	1.224	0.9961	No
State Median Wage (Schleswig-Holstein)	-2.582	0.0969*	Yes
State Median Wage (Hamburg)	-2.093	0.2472	No
State Median Wage (Lower Saxony)	-2.702	0.0738*	Yes
State Median Wage (Bremen)	-2.406	0.1400	No
State Median Wage (North-Rhine-Westfalia)	-2.644	0.0842*	Yes
State Median Wage (Hessen)	-1.882	0.3407	No
State Median Wage (Rheinland-Pfalz)	-2.058	0.2619	No
State Median Wage (Baden-Wuerttemberg)	-2.726	0.0697*	Yes
State Median Wage (Bavaria)	-3.193	0.0204**	Yes
State Median Wage (Saarland)	-1.420	0.5727	No
State Median Wage (Berlin)	-4.794	0.0001***	Yes
State Median Wage (Brandenburg)	-6.201	0.0000***	Yes
State Median Wage (Mecklenburg-Vorpommern)	-5.637	0.0000***	Yes
State Median Wage (Saxony)	-6.531	0.0000***	Yes
State Median Wage (Saxony-Anhalt)	-4.830	0.0000***	Yes
State Median Wage (Thuringia)	-4.776	0.0001***	Yes
State Unemployment Rate (Schleswig-Holstein)	-1.648	0.4581	No
State Unemployment Rate (Hamburg)	-1.600	0.4836	No
State Unemployment Rate (Lower Saxony)	-1.135	0.7011	No
State Unemployment Rate (Bremen)	-2.056	0.2627	No
State Unemployment Rate (North-Rhine-Westfalia)	-2.137	0.2299	No
State Unemployment Rate (Hessen)	-2.048	0.2660	No

Table B.5: Dickey-Fuller Test for Stationarity, Original Variables - Continued

Variable	Test Statistic τ	P-Value	Reject H_0?
State Unemployment Rate (Rheinland-Pfalz)	-1.653	0.4554	No
State Unemployment Rate (Baden-Wuerttemberg	-1.874	0.3444	No
State Unemployment Rate (Bavaria)	-1.410	0.5772	No
State Unemployment Rate (Saarland)	-1.105	0.7130	No
State Unemployment Rate (Berlin)	-2.008	0.2829	No
State Unemployment Rate (Brandenburg)	-1.325	0.6179	No
State Unemployment Rate (Mecklenburg-Vorpommern)	-1.328	0.6163	No
State Unemployment Rate (Saxony)	-1.569	0.4992	No
State Unemployment Rate (Saxony-Anhalt)	-1.536	0.5154	No
State Unemployment Rate (Thuringia)	-1.049	0.7349	No
Number of Apprenticeship Places	-0.958	0.7682	No
National Unemployment Rate	-1.459	0.5534	No
Relative Youth Cohort Size	-0.917	0.7824	No

Notes: No tests could be conducted for Postal Services, Professional Education and Security Services because of too few observations. As the GSOEP contains no observations for roofers, test results are not displayed here.
*** p<0.01, ** p<0.05, * p<0.1

Sources: GSOEP, FSO, minimum wage regulations; author's calculations

Table B.6: Dickey-Fuller Test for Stationarity, First Differences of Variables
H_0: Time Series is Instationary

Variable	Test Statistic τ	P-Value	Reject H_0?
Minimum Wage (Main Construction Trades, West)	-4.256	0.0005***	Yes
Minimum Wage (Main Construction Trades, East)	-3.749	0.0035***	Yes
Minimum Wage (Electrical Trades, West)	-3.778	0.0031***	Yes
Minimum Wage (Electrical Trades, East)	-5.264	0.0000***	Yes
Minimum Wage (Painting & Varnishing, West)	-2.824	0.0549*	Yes
Minimum Wage (Painting & Varnishing, East)	-2.641	0.0848*	Yes
Minimum Wage (Building Cleaning, West)	-2.597	0.0937*	Yes
Minimum Wage (Hard Coal Mining, West)	-4.292	0.0005***	Yes
Minimum Wage (Hard Coal Mining, East)	–	–	–
Minimum Wage (Waste Management, West)	–	–	–
Minimum Wage (Waste Management, East)	–	–	–
State Median Wage (Schleswig-Holstein)	-5.171	0.0000***	Yes
State Median Wage (Hamburg)	-6.181	0.0000***	Yes
State Median Wage (Lower Saxony)	-4.023	0.0013***	Yes
State Median Wage (Bremen)	-7.193	0.0000***	Yes
State Median Wage (North-Rhine-Westfalia)	-2.184	0.2122	No

Table B.6: Dickey-Fuller Test for Stationarity, First Differences of Variables - Continued

Variable	Test Statistic τ	P-Value	Reject H_0?
State Median Wage (Hessen)	-4.332	0.0004***	Yes
State Median Wage (Rheinland-Pfalz)	-5.009	0.0000***	Yes
State Median Wage (Baden-Wuerttemberg)	-3.094	0.0270**	Yes
State Median Wage (Bavaria)	-3.571	0.0063**'	Yes
State Median Wage (Saarland)	-1.789	0.3860	No
State Median Wage (Berlin)	-4.666	0.0001***	Yes
State Median Wage (Brandenburg)	-2.156	0.2225	No
State Median Wage (Mecklenburg-Vorpommern)	-3.435	0.0098***	Yes
State Median Wage (Saxony)	-2.563	0.1009*	Yes
State Median Wage (Saxony-Anhalt)	-2.746	0.0665*	Yes
State Median Wage (Thuringia)	-3.658	0.0047***	Yes
State Unemployment Rate (Schleswig-Holstein)	-3.265	0.0165**	Yes
State Unemployment Rate (Hamburg)	-3.130	0.0244**	Yes
State Unemployment Rate (Lower Saxony)	-3.230	0.0183**	Yes
State Unemployment Rate (Bremen)	-3.379	0.0117**	Yes
State Unemployment Rate (North-Rhine-Westfalia)	-3.118	0.0252**	Yes
State Unemployment Rate (Hessen)	-2.704	0.0734*	Yes
State Unemployment Rate (Rheinland-Pfalz)	-2.943	0.0406**	Yes
State Unemployment Rate (Baden-Wuerttemberg)	-2.958	0.0390**	Yes
State Unemployment Rate (Bavaria)	-2.960	0.0388**	Yes
State Unemployment Rate (Saarland)	-3.399	0.0110**	Yes
State Unemployment Rate (Berlin)	-2.902	0.0451**	Yes
State Unemployment Rate (Brandenburg)	-4.215	0.0006***	Yes
State Unemployment Rate (Mecklenburg-Vorpommern)	-3.793	0.0030***	Yes
State Unemployment Rate (Saxony)	-4.029	0.0013***	Yes
State Unemployment Rate (Saxony-Anhalt)	-3.866	0.0023***	Yes
State Unemployment Rate (Thuringia)	-4.711	0.0001***	Yes
Number of Apprenticeship Places	-3.246	0.0175**	Yes
National Unemployment Rate	-2.918	0.0433**	Yes
Relative Youth Cohort Size	-3.750	0.0031***	Yes

Notes: No tests could be conducted for Postal Services, Professional Education and Security Services because of too few observations. As the GSOEP contains no observations for roofers, test results are not displayed here.
*** p<0.01, ** p<0.05, * p<0.1

Sources: GSOEP, FSO, minimum wage regulations; author's calculations

Table B.7: Cross-Correlation Table 2, Minimum Wages Only

Variables	(1)	(2)	(3)	(4)	(5)	(6)	(7)	(8)
(Δ Minimum Wage)$_t$ (1)	1.000							
(Δ Minimum Wage)$_{t-1}$ (2)	-0.146	1.000						
(Δ Minimum Wage)$_{t-2}$ (3)	-0.060	-0.170	1.000					
(Δ Minimum Wage)$_{t-3}$ (4)	-0.028	-0.050	-0.192	1.000				
(Δ Kaitz Index)$_t$ (5)	0.984	-0.150	-0.066	-0.028	1.000			
(Δ Kaitz Index)$_{t-1}$ (6)	-0.139	0.982	-0.174	-0.056	-0.148	1.000		
(Δ Kaitz Index)$_{t-2}$ (7)	-0.058	-0.164	0.982	-0.186	-0.066	-0.174	1.000	
(Δ Kaitz Index)$_{t-3}$ (8)	-0.023	-0.048	-0.181	0.982	-0.024	-0.057	-0.180	1.000

Sources: GSOEP, FSO, minimum wage regulations; author's calculations

C Regression Supplements

Table C.1: Collinearity Diagnostics, Regression Using Absolute Minimum Wages

Variable	VIF	$\sqrt{VIF}$	Tolerance	R-squared
Educational Status	1.20	1.10	0.8340	0.1660
(Δ Minimum Wage)$_t$	1.08	1.04	0.9277	0.0723
(Δ Minimum Wage)$_{t-1}$	1.11	1.05	0.8988	0.1012
(Δ Minimum Wage)$_{t-2}$	1.13	1.06	0.8818	0.1182
(Δ Minimum Wage)$_{t-3}$	1.07	1.04	0.9319	0.0681
Sex	1.20	1.09	0.8367	0.1633
Nationality	1.06	1.03	0.9427	0.0573
Lower to Medium Secondary School Degree	1.08	1.04	0.9293	0.0707
Age	1.21	1.10	0.8270	0.1730
(Δ State Unemployment Rate)$_{t-1}$	1.04	1.02	0.9622	0.0378
(Δ Household Income)$_{t-1}$	1.01	1.00	0.9934	0.0066
(Δ Number of Apprenticeship Places)$_{t-1}$	1.23	1.11	0.8128	0.1872
(Δ Relative Youth Cohort Size)$_{t-1}$	1.32	1.15	0.7583	0.2417
Time	1.46	1.21	0.6827	0.3173
Economic Sector According to NACE	1.17	1.08	0.8567	0.1433
Mean VIF	1.16			

Sources: GSOEP, FSO, minimum wage regulations, author's calculations

Table C.2: Collinearity Diagnostics, Regression Using Relative Minimum Wages

Variable	VIF	$\sqrt{VIF}$	Tolerance	R-squared
Educational Status	1.20	1.10	0.8338	0.1662
(Δ Kaitz Index)$_t$	1.08	1.04	0.9252	0.0748
(Δ Kaitz Index)$_{t-1}$	1.12	1.06	0.8929	0.1071
(Δ Kaitz Index)$_{t-2}$	1.13	1.06	0.8848	0.1152
(Δ Kaitz Index)$_{t-3}$	1.06	1.03	0.9397	0.0603
Sex	1.19	1.09	0.8373	0.1627
Nationality	1.06	1.03	0.9424	0.0576
Lower to Medium Secondary School Degree	1.08	1.04	0.9296	0.0704
Age	1.21	1.10	0.8268	0.1732
(Δ State Unemployment Rate)$_{t-1}$	1.04	1.02	0.9624	0.0376
(Δ Household Income)$_{t-1}$	1.01	1.00	0.9933	0.0067
(Δ Number of Apprenticeship Places)$_{t-1}$	1.23	1.11	0.8133	0.1867
(Δ Relative Youth Cohort Size)$_{t-1}$	1.32	1.15	0.7583	0.2417
Time	1.46	1.21	0.6846	0.3154
Economic Sector According to NACE	1.17	1.08	0.8568	0.1432
Mean VIF	1.16			

Sources: GSOEP, FSO, minimum wage regulations; author's calculations

Table C.3: Collinearity Diagnostics, Regression Using ISCED Level (Modified)

Variable	VIF	$\sqrt{VIF}$	Tolerance	R-squared
ISCED Level (Modified)	1.34	1.16	0.7451	0.2549
(Δ Kaitz Index)$_{t-3}$	1.07	1.03	0.9337	0.0663
(Δ Kaitz Index)$_{t-4}$	1.09	1.05	0.9133	0.0867
(Δ Kaitz Index)$_{t-5}$	1.07	1.04	0.9308	0.0692
Sex	1.03	1.02	0.9684	0.0274
Nationality	1.05	1.02	0.9567	0.0433
Lower to Medium Secondary School Degree	1.06	1.03	0.9464	0.0536
Age	1.34	1.16	0.7477	0.2423
(Δ State Unemployment Rate)$_{t-4}$	1.06	1.03	0.9470	0.0530
(Δ Number of Apprenticeship Places)$_{t-4}$	1.21	1.10	0.8270	0.1730
(Δ Relative Youth Cohort Size)$_{t-4}$	1.37	1.17	0.7289	0.2711
Time	1.43	1.20	0.6992	0.3008
Mean VIF	1.18			

Sources: GSOEP, FSO, minimum wage regulations; author's calculations

Table C.4: Results of Basic OLS Estimation

	(1)
Dep. Variable: Educational Status	Panel OLS
$(\Delta \text{ Minimum Wage})_t$	0.00295
	(0.00216)
$(\Delta \text{ Minimum Wage})_{t-1}$	0.00611**
	(0.00262)
$(\Delta \text{ Minimum Wage})_{t-2}$	0.00691**
	(0.00313)
$(\Delta \text{ Minimum Wage})_{t-3}$	0.00346
	(0.00415)
Constant	1.336***
	(0.0280)
Observations	8,062
Controls	No
Year Effects	Yes
Sector Effects	No
R-squared	0.126

Standard errors in parentheses; *** p<0.01, ** p<0.05, * p<0.1

Sources: GSOEP, FSO, minimum wage regulations; author's calculations

Table C.5: Wald Test Results for Baseline Regression Estimates

Test	Test Statistic X^2	P-Value
`diff_kaitz = diff_kaitzl1 = diff_kaitzl2`	1.11	0.5730
`diff_kaitz = diff_kaitzl1`	0.92	0.3366
`diff_kaitz = diff_kaitzl2`	0.01	0.9243
`1.schooldeg_sec = 2.schooldeg_sec`	44.55	0.0000

Sources: GSOEP, FSO, minimum wage regulations; author's calculations

Table C.6: Mean Predicted Probabilities, Baseline Regression without Controls

Cut-Off Value	Mean Prediction	Std. Err.	P-Value
$(\Delta \text{ Kaitz Index})_t$ = -1	0.8780901	0.0375747	0.0000
$(\Delta \text{ Kaitz Index})_t$ = -0.5	0.9315627	0.0132876	0.0000
$(\Delta \text{ Kaitz Index})_t$ = 0	0.9628811	0.0042972	0.0000
$(\Delta \text{ Kaitz Index})_t$ = 0.5	0.9802817	0.0039015	0.0000
$(\Delta \text{ Kaitz Index})_t$ = 1	0.9896481	0.0036131	0.0000
$(\Delta \text{ Kaitz Index})_{t-1}$ = -1	0.7774647	0.0809821	0.0000
$(\Delta \text{ Kaitz Index})_{t-1}$ = -0.5	0.9047065	0.0226495	0.0000
$(\Delta \text{ Kaitz Index})_{t-1}$ = 0	0.9635193	0.0042258	0.0000
$(\Delta \text{ Kaitz Index})_{t-1}$ = 0.5	0.9867564	0.0034493	0.0000
$(\Delta \text{ Kaitz Index})_{t-1}$ = 1	0.9952938	0.0022942	0.0000
$(\Delta \text{ Kaitz Index})_{t-2}$ = -1	0.854659	0.0679212	0.0000
$(\Delta \text{ Kaitz Index})_{t-2}$ = -0.5	0.9255126	0.020632	0.0000
$(\Delta \text{ Kaitz Index})_{t-2}$ = 0	0.9637389	0.0041992	0.0000
$(\Delta \text{ Kaitz Index})_{t-2}$ = 0.5	0.9828498	0.0049981	0.0000
$(\Delta \text{ Kaitz Index})_{t-2}$ = 1	0.9920083	0.0044578	0.0000

Sources: GSOEP, FSO, minimum wage regulations; author's calculations

Table C.7: Mean Predicted Probabilities, Baseline Regression with Controls

Cut-Off Value	Mean Prediction	Std. Err.	P-Value
$(\Delta \text{ Kaitz Index})_t$ = -1	0.8723989	0.042287	0.0000
$(\Delta \text{ Kaitz Index})_t$ = -0.5	0.9236863	0.0167996	0.0000
$(\Delta \text{ Kaitz Index})_t$ = 0	0.9565054	0.0064985	0.0000
$(\Delta \text{ Kaitz Index})_t$ = 0.5	0.9762543	0.0058742	0.0000
$(\Delta \text{ Kaitz Index})_t$ = 1	0.9875075	0.0054605	0.0000
$(\Delta \text{ Kaitz Index})_{t-1}$ = -1	0.8205984	0.0664455	0.0000
$(\Delta \text{ Kaitz Index})_{t-1}$ = -0.5	0.9079506	0.0225749	0.0000
$(\Delta \text{ Kaitz Index})_{t-1}$ = 0	0.9569776	0.0064285	0.0000
$(\Delta \text{ Kaitz Index})_{t-1}$ = 0.5	0.9814462	0.0054653	0.0000
$(\Delta \text{ Kaitz Index})_{t-1}$ = 1	0.9924974	0.0041403	0.0000
$(\Delta \text{ Kaitz Index})_{t-2}$ = -1	0.8687834	0.0552221	0.0000
$(\Delta \text{ Kaitz Index})_{t-2}$ = -0.5	0.9229905	0.0203289	0.0000
$(\Delta \text{ Kaitz Index})_{t-2}$ = 0	0.9571007	0.0064146	0.0000
$(\Delta \text{ Kaitz Index})_{t-2}$ = 0.5	0.9771677	0.0067969	0.0000
$(\Delta \text{ Kaitz Index})_{t-2}$ = 1	0.9883046	0.0065485	0.0000

Sources: GSOEP, FSO, minimum wage regulations; author's calculations

Table C.8: Mean Predicted Probabilities for Subgroups 1

Subgroup	Cut-Off Value (Δ Kaitz Index)$_t$	Apprenticeship Probability	P-Value
	-1	0.844482	0.000
	-0.5	0.9047568	0.000
Females	0	0.9445128	0.000
	0.5	0.969076	0.000
	1	0.9834186	0.000
	-1	0.8905974	0.000
	-0.5	0.9354285	0.000
Males	0	0.963596	0.000
	0.5	0.9802862	0.000
	1	0.9896802	0.000
	-1	0.4164871	0.004
	-0.5	0.5656611	0.000
No Secondary Degree	0	0.7041703	0.000
	0.5	0.8152759	0.000
	1	0.8931681	0.000
	-1	0.7692991	0.000
	-0.5	0.8621307	0.000
Lower Secondary Degree	0	0.9230562	0.000
	0.5	0.9592278	0.000
	1	0.9791669	0.000
	-1	0.9421895	0.000
	-0.5	0.9699271	0.000
Medium Secondary Degree	0	0.9848204	0.000
	0.5	0.9924801	0.000
	1	0.9963143	0.000
	-1	0.8968816	0.000
	-0.5	0.9416749	0.000
German	0	0.9684693	0.000
	0.5	0.9835493	0.000
	1	0.9916484	0.000
	-1	0.6598152	0.000
	-0.5	0.7731029	0.000
Non-German	0	0.8589531	0.000
	0.5	0.9176154	0.000
	1	0.9543065	0.000

Sources: GSOEP, FSO, minimum wage regulations; author's calculations

Table C.9: Mean Predicted Probabilities for Subgroups 2

Subgroup	Cut-Off Value (Δ Kaitz Index)$_{t-1}$	Apprenticeship Probability	P-Value
	-1	0.7852221	0.0000
	-0.5	0.8860486	0.0000
Females	0	0.945082	0.0000
	0.5	0.9756253	0.0000
	1	0.9898907	0.0000
	-1	0.8445419	0.0000
	-0.5	0.9217548	0.0000
Males	0	0.9639618	0.0000
	0.5	0.9846005	0.0000
	1	0.9937964	0.0000
	-1	0.3117697	0.031
	-0.5	0.5112339	0.0000
No Secondary Degree	0	0.70548	0.0000
	0.5	0.849072	0.0000
	1	0.9323074	0.0000
	-1	0.680122	0.0000
	-0.5	0.832444	0.0000
Lower Secondary Degree	0	0.9235951	0.0000
	0.5	0.9683973	0.0000
	1	0.9876764	0.0000
	-1	0.9090999	0.0000
	-0.5	0.9617595	0.0000
Medium SecondaryDegree	0	0.9849443	0.0000
	0.5	0.9942792	0.0000
	1	0.9978614	0.0000
	-1	0.84918	0.0000
	-0.5	0.9283005	0.0000
German	0	0.968922	0.0000
	0.5	0.987399	0.0000
	1	0.9951162	0.0000
	-1	0.5627633	0.0000
	-0.5	0.7353056	0.0000
Non-German	0	0.860247	0.0000
	0.5	0.9343211	0.0000
	1	0.9717722	0.0000

Sources: GSOEP, FSO, minimum wage regulations; author's calculations

Table C.10: Mean Predicted Probabilities for Subgroups 3

Subgroup	Cut-Off Value (Δ Kaitz Index)$_{t-2}$	Apprenticeship Probability	P-Value
	-1	0.8404005	0.0000
	-0.5	0.90398	0.0000
Females	0	0.945267	0.0000
	0.5	0.9702476	0.0000
	1	0.98447	0.0000
	-1	0.8874654	0.0000
	-0.5	0.9348481	0.0000
Males	0	0.9641	0.0000
	0.5	0.9810456	0.0000
	1	0.9903415	0.0000
	-1	0.4078323	0.013
	-0.5	0.5627327	0.0000
No Secondary Degree	0	0.706605	0.0000
	0.5	0.8207435	0.0000
	1	0.8991293	0.0000
	-1	0.7623172	0.0000
	-0.5	0.8603269	0.0000
Lower Secondary Degree	0	0.9298962	0.0000
	0.5	0.9607387	0.0000
	1	0.9805292	0.0000
	-1	0.9397661	0.0000
	-0.5	0.9694403	0.0000
Medium Secondary Degree	0	0.9849995	0.0000
	0.5	0.9927832	0.0000
	1	0.9965666	0.0000
	-1	0.8936314	0.0000
	-0.5	0.9410558	0.0000
German	0	0.9688954	0.0000
	0.5	0.9841889	0.0000
	1	0.9921812	0.0000
	-1	0.6516597	0.0000
	-0.5	0.7715319	0.0000
Non-German	0	0.8607204	0.0000
	0.5	0.9205717	0.0000
	1	0.9571272	0.0000

Sources: GSOEP, FSO, minimum wage regulations; author's calculations

Table C.11: Alternative Regression 2b, Estimation of ISCED Level (Modified) without Year Effects

Dep. Variable: ISCED Level (Modified)	(1) GLS	(2) GLS	(3) OL	(4) OL	(5) FE OL	(6) FE OL
$(\Delta \text{ Kaitz Index})_{t-3}$	0.192***	0.218***	2.141***	1.766***	2.450***	2.323***
	(0.0196)	(0.0213)	(0.324)	(0.471)	(0.414)	(0.654)
$(\Delta \text{ Kaitz Index})_{t-4}$	0.344***	0.416***	3.425***	3.129***	3.911***	4.332***
	(0.0330)	(0.0292)	(0.454)	(0.575)	(0.639)	(1.067)
$(\Delta \text{ Kaitz Index})_{t-5}$	0.415***	0.431***	4.623***	3.984***	5.417***	5.029***
	(0.0457)	(0.0286)	(0.605)	(0.592)	(0.994)	(1.367)
Sex: Female		0.127***		0.767***		
		(0.00155)		(0.172)		
Nationality: Non-German		-0.0447***		-0.573**		
		(0.00539)		(0.277)		
Nationality						-16.10***
						(0.701)
Secondary Degree: Lower		1.219***		9.258***		
		(0.0178)		(1.295)		
Secondary Degree: Medium		1.168***		8.994***		
		(0.0178)		(1.296)		
Lower to Medium Secondary School Degree						15.09***
						(0.592)
$(\Delta \text{ State Unemployment Rate})_{t-4}$		-0.0101***		-0.151***		-0.148***
		(0.000332)		(0.0485)		(0.0480)
$(\Delta \text{ Number of Apprenticeship Places})_{t-4}$		0.000688***		0.00776***		0.0140***
		(0.0000260)		(0.00186)		(0.00237)
$(\Delta \text{ Relative Youth Cohort Size})_{t-4}$		-0.0683***		-0.712***		-1.234***
		(0.000181)		(0.110)		(0.171)
Constant	2.432***	1.188***				
	(0.00157)	(0.0178)				
Observations	9,650	3,734	11,324	4,251	5,400	1,970
Controls	No	Yes	No	Yes	No	Yes
Year Effects	No	No	No	No	No	No
Sector Effects	No	No	No	No	No	No
Pseudo R-squared					0.0331	0.1286

Standard errors in parentheses; *** p<0.01, ** p<0.05, * p<0.1

Notes: The FE OL model cannot deal with factor variables for what reason the effects on nationality, school degrees and time are based on the regular indicators or continous variables respectively.

Sources: GSOEP, FSO, minimum wage regulations; author's calculations

Table C.12: Alternative Regression 5b, Separation by School Degrees (Linear Approach)

	No Secondary Degree		Lower Degree		Medium Degree	
	(1)	(2)	(3)	(4)	(5)	(6)
Dep. Variable: Educational Status	GLS	GLS	GLS	GLS	GLS	GLS
(Δ Kaitz Index)$_t$	-0.0210	0.0777***	0.0828	0.0554***	–	0.0976***
	(0.0487)	(0.0856)	(0.00708)	(0.00684)	–	(0.00171)
(Δ Kaitz Index)$_{t-1}$	-0.124	0.0564	0.130***	0.132***	0.0152***	0.121***
	(0.101)	(0.188)	(0.0113)	(0.00991)	(0.00170)	(0.00213)
(Δ Kaitz Index)$_{t-2}$	-0.116	-1.256***	0.124***	0.135***	0.00418	0.0585***
	(0.160)	(0.214)	(0.0166)	(0.00935)	(0.00712)	(0.00346)
(Δ Kaitz Index)$_{t-3}$			0.0949***	0.0957***	-0.106***	-0.164***
			(0.0248)	(0.0147)	(0.0285)	(0.0133)
Sex: Female		0.332***		-0.0545***		-0.0161***
		(0.0515)		(0.00608)		(0.00110)
Nationality: Non-German		0.372***		-0.168***		-0.0353***
		(0.0848)		(0.0113)		(0.00156)
(Δ State Unemployment Rate)$_{t-1}$		-0.0283		0.0156***		-0.00167***
		(0.0418)		(0.00104)		(0.000153)
(Δ Number of Apprenticeship		-0.00206		0.00107**		-0.000293***
Places)$_{t-1}$		(0.00171)		(0.000427)		(0.0000735)
(Δ Relative Youth Cohort Size)$_{t-1}$		-0.270***		2.227***		0.666***
		(0.0576)		(0.211)		(0.0414)
Constant	0.907***	0.600***	0.848***	0.532***	0.951***	0.860***
	(0.0158)	(0.0982)	(0.0116)	(0.0416)	(0.00495)	(0.00763)
Observations	299	69	2,189	1,203	4,023	2,440
Controls	No	Yes	No	Yes	No	Yes
Year Effects	Yes	Yes	Yes	Yes	Yes	Yes
Sector Effects	No	No	No	No	No	No

Standard errors in parentheses; *** p<0.01, ** p<0.05, * p<0.1

Sources: GSOEP, FSO, minimum wage regulations; author's calculations

Table C.13: Alternative Regression 5c, Separation by Required Education

	No Education or Orientation		Introduction or Professional Education	
	(1)	(2)	(3)	(4)
Dep. Variable: Educational Status	GLS	GLS	MIL	MIL
$(\Delta$ Kaitz Index$)_t$	0.108***	0.0834***	0.986	2.239***
	(0.0199)	(0.000676)	(0.867)	(0.476)
$(\Delta$ Kaitz Index$)_{t-1}$	0.341***	0.130***	3.497**	3.334***
	(0.0438)	(0.000966)	(1.418)	(0.642)
$(\Delta$ Kaitz Index$)_{t-2}$	0.317***	0.0723***	2.201	2.050***
	(0.0563)	(0.00210)	(2.158)	(0.652)
$(\Delta$ Kaitz Index$)_{t-3}$	-0.0623	-0.0662***	-0.380	0.267
	(0.0452)	(0.00483)	(3.523)	(0.850)
Constant	0.0140**	0.0181	-2.027***	4.089***
	(0.00584)	(0.0193)	(0.263)	(0.194)
Individual Intercept (Std. Dev.)			1.462***	1.233***
			(0.107)	(0.0454)
Observations	510	4,471	1,014	5,669
Number of Groups			715	2,757
Year Effects	Yes	Yes	Yes	Yes
Sector Effects	No	No	No	No

Standard errors in parentheses; *** p<0.01, ** p<0.05, * p<0.1

Sources: GSOEP, FSO, minimum wage regulations; author's calculations

Table C.14: Alternative Regression 6, Age Groups

	Age 17-20		Age 21-22		Age 23-24	
	(1)	(2)	(3)	(4)	(5)	(6)
Dep. Variable: Educational Status	GLS	GLS	GLS	GLS	GLS	GLS
$(\Delta$ Kaitz Index$)_t$	–	0.0594***	0.0971***	0.0898***	0.252***	0.178***
	–	(0.000764)	(0.0154)	(0.0147)	(0.0200)	(0.0232)
$(\Delta$ Kaitz Index$)_{t-1}$	0.0182***	0.0317***	0.00276	-0.00174	0.277***	0.238***
	(0.000649)	(0.00171)	(0.0158)	(0.0133)	(0.0270)	(0.0257)
$(\Delta$ Kaitz Index$)_{t-2}$	0.00742***	0.0568***	-0.0266*	-0.0365***	0.0332	-0.0682**
	(0.00165)	(0.00263)	(0.0149)	(0.0125)	(0.0202)	(0.0271)
$(\Delta$ Kaitz Index$)_{t-3}$	0.0210**	0.0745***	-0.0806***	-0.102***	0.0383***	-0.0236
	(0.00881)	(0.00660)	(0.0135)	(0.0125)	(0.0132)	(0.0172)
Sex: Female		-0.00927***		-0.0910***		0.0989***
		(0.000284)		(0.00292)		(0.0176)
Nationality: Non-German		-0.155***		-0.0531***		0.186***
		(0.00218)		(0.0118)		(0.0288)
Secondary Degree: Lower		0.119***		-0.292***		0.219***
		(0.0132)		(0.00575)		(0.0264)
Secondary Degree: Medium		0.160***		-0.207***		0.373***
		(0.0132)		(0.00334)		(0.0225)
$(\Delta$ State Unemployment Rate$)_{t-1}$		0.00106***		0.0300***		-0.0263***
		(0.0000468)		(0.00152)		(0.00116)
$(\Delta$ Number of Apprenticeship Places$)_{t-1}$		-0.00142***		0.00292***		-0.00243***
		(0.000159)		(0.000116)		(0.000106)
$(\Delta$ Relative Youth Cohort Size$)_{t-1}$		0.209***		0.0781		2.562***
		(0.0173)		(0.116)		(0.171)
Constant	1.000***	0.839***	0.595***	1.036***	0.0911***	0.0259
	(0.0000000108)	(0.0141)	(0.0243)	(0.0231)	(0.00775)	(0.0311)
Observations	3,748	2,062	868	562	621	347
Controls	No	Yes	No	Yes	No	Yes
Year Effects	Yes	Yes	Yes	Yes	Yes	Yes
Sector Effects	No	No	No	No	No	No

Standard errors in parentheses ; *** p<0.01, ** p<0.05, * p<0.1

Sources: GSOEP, FSO, minimum wage regulations; author's calculations

Table C.15: Alternative Regression 7, Household Income as a Control

Dep. Variable: Educational Status	(1) GLS	(2) CL	(3) MIL
$(\Delta$ Kaitz Index$)_t$	0.104***	0.383	1.403***
	(0.00105)	(0.786)	(0.424)
$(\Delta$ Kaitz Index$)_{t-1}$	0.159***	-0.218	2.098***
	(0.00206)	(0.850)	(0.535)
$(\Delta$ Kaitz Index$)_{t-2}$	0.108***	-0.125	1.569***
	(0.00376)	(0.621)	(0.565)
$(\Delta$ Kaitz Index$)_{t-3}$	-0.0392***	-0.492	0.224
	(0.0110)	(0.554)	(0.678)
Sex: Female	-0.0241***		-0.442**
	(0.000418)		(0.214)
Nationality: Non-German	-0.108***	0.114	-1.428***
	(0.00158)	(0.808)	(0.315)
Secondary Degree: Lower	0.162***		1.591***
	(0.00302)		(0.513)
Secondary Degree: Medium	0.237***	1.712	3.140***
	(0.00232)	(1.761)	(0.516)
$(\Delta$ State Unemployment Rate$)_{t-1}$	0.00265***	0.0537	0.0424
	(0.0000814)	(0.0850)	(0.0538)
$(\Delta$ Number of Apprenticeship Places$)_{t-1}$	-0.000305***	-0.0561***	-0.0065**
	(0.0000129)	(0.0174)	(0.0022)
$(\Delta$ Relative Youth Cohort Size$)_{t-1}$	1.030***	78.44***	0.299*
	(0.0252)	(14.96)	(0.165)
$(\Delta$ Household Income$)_{t-1}$	-0.00245***	-0.0335	-0.0134
	(0.000119)	(0.0579)	(0.0501)
Constant	0.573***		1.289
	(0.00467)		(0.501)
Individual Intercept (Std. Dev.)			3.027***
			(0.171)
Observations	3,753	800	4,542
Number of Groups			2,040
Year Effects	Yes	Yes	No
Sector Effects	No	No	No

Standard errors in parentheses; *** p<0.01, ** p<0.05, * p<0.1
Sources: GSOEP, FSO, minimum wage regulations; author's calculations

Table C.16: Alternative Regression 8, Excluding States with Instationary First Differences of Median Wages

Dep. Variable: Educational Status	Baseline Regression			Excluding States		
	(1)	(2)	(3)	(4)	(5)	(6)
	GLS	CL	MIL	GLS	CL	MIL
$(\Delta$ Kaitz Index$)_t$	0.0437***	0.553	1.316***	0.0498***	0.433	1.087***
	(0.00453)	(0.627)	(0.340)	(0.00414)	(0.765)	(0.402)
$(\Delta$ Kaitz Index$)_{t-1}$	0.0629***	0.291	2.094***	0.0761***	0.244	2.482***
	(0.00647)	(0.715)	(0.480)	(0.00654)	(0.756)	(0.583)
$(\Delta$ Kaitz Index$)_{t-2}$	0.0512***	0.0999	1.555***	0.0731***	0.284	2.048***
	(0.00918)	(0.547)	(0.557)	(0.00963)	(0.689)	(0.691)
$(\Delta$ Kaitz Index$)_{t-3}$	0.00240	-0.351	0.135	0.0404***	0.0596	0.980
	(0.0168)	(0.521)	(0.685)	(0.0146)	(0.657)	(0.837)
Constant	0.934***		3.216***	0.918***		3.293***
	(0.00120)		(0.267)	(0.00499)		(0.142)
Individual Intercept (Std. Dev.)			1.215***			3.233***
			(0.0582)			(0.139)
Observations	6,571	1,352	8,062	4,855	971	5,980
Number of Groups			3,682			2,745
Controls	No	No	No	No	No	No
Year Effects	Yes	Yes	Yes	Yes	Yes	No
Sector Effects	No	No	No	No	No	No
Pseudo R-squared		0.348			0.358	

Standard errors in parentheses; *** p<0.01, ** p<0.05, * p<0.1

Sources: GSOEP, FSO, minimum wage regulations; author's calculations

D Graphical Illustrations

Figure D.1: State Median Wages and State Unemployment Rates, 1990/1991-2013

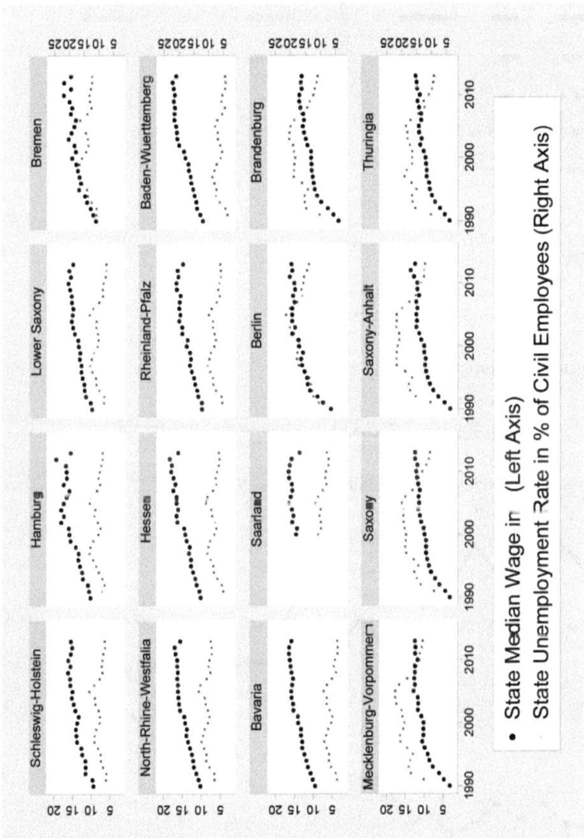

Sources: GSOEP, FSO; author's figure

Figure D.2: Scatterplot of ISCED Level (Modified) against Minimum Wages, Youth Aged 17-24

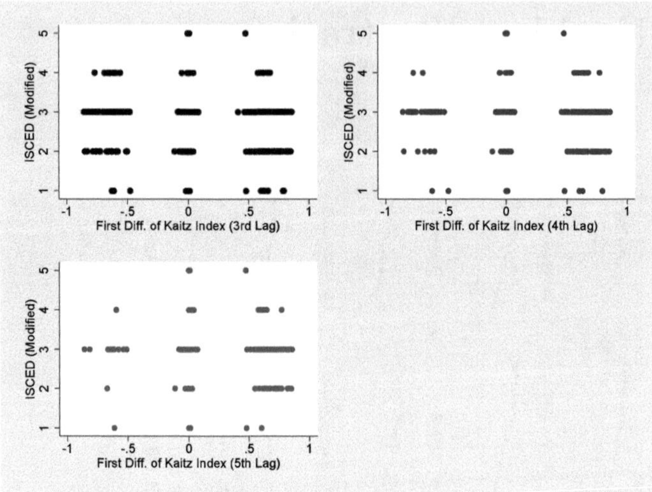

Sources: GSOEP, FSO, minimum wage regulations; author's figure

Figure D.3: Mean Ages of Apprentices and Unskilled Workers, Youth Aged 17-24

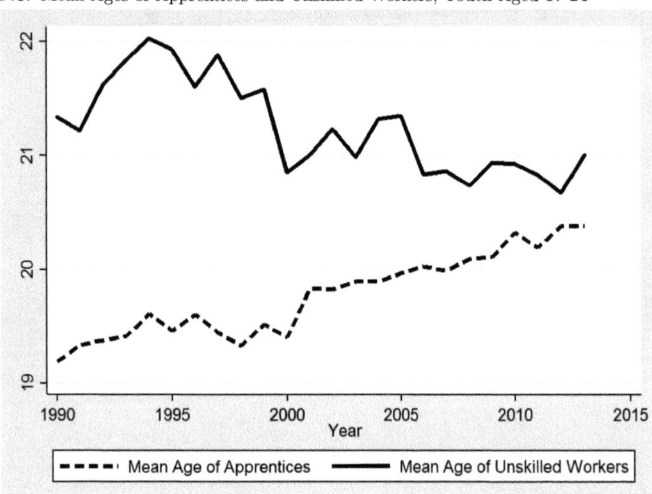

Source: GSOEP; author's figure

MIX
Papier aus verantwortungsvollen Quellen
Paper from responsible sources
FSC® C105338

If you have any concerns about our products,
you can contact us on
ProductSafety@springernature.com

In case Publisher is established outside the EU,
the EU authorized representative is:
Springer Nature Customer Service Center GmbH
Europaplatz 3, 69115 Heidelberg, Germany

Printed by Libri Plureos GmbH
in Hamburg, Germany